Writing in the Margins

A FIELD GUIDE TO ACADEMIC WRITING

STEPHEN GILBERT BROWN

Director, Program in Writing & Rhetoric
UNLV

FOUNTAINHEAD PRESS

Cover design by Adam Novak
Text design by Patricia Bracken

© 2007 Stephen G. Brown.

All rights reserved. No part of this book may be reproduced or utilized in any form or by any means, electronic or mechanical, including photocopying and recording, or by any information storage and retrieval system without written permission from the publisher.

Books may be purchased for educational purposes.

For information, please call or write:

1-800-586-0330

Fountainhead Press
100 W. Southlake Blvd. Suite 142, #350
Southlake, TX 76092

Web site: www.fountainheadpress.com
Email: customerservice@fountainheadpress.com

ISBN 978-1-59871-168-4
Printed in the United States of America

DEDICATION

This book is dedicated to:

Professor John Clark

(University of South Florida)

who taught me how to write,

and to

Shellmarie,

who brings happiness to all the rest.

STEPHEN GILBERT BROWN

Biographical Sketch

In addition to *Writing in the Margins*, Stephen Gilbert Brown is also the author of the award-winning *Words in the Wilderness: Critical Literacy in the Borderlands* (SUNY 2000), *Ethnography Unbound: From Theory Shock to Critical Praxis* (SUNY 2004) and *The Gardens of Desire: Marcel Proust and the Fugitive Sublime* (SUNY 2004). He is currently at work on two books, *Plato and the Art of Revenge* (SUNY P, under review) and *Composing the Eco Wars: Writing, Literacy, and the Environment* (McGraw Hill, under review).

He has published numerous articles on writing and literacy in *College Literature, Review of Education*, and *Journal of Advanced Composition*. Spring 2005, he received the prestigious Barrick Scholar Award at UNLV. He received his BA in English from U.C., Santa Barbara, his MA and PhD in Rhetoric/Composition from the University of South Florida. He is currently Associate Professor of English, Director of the Composition Program, at University of Nevada, Las Vegas.

ACKNOWLEDGEMENTS

For the guidance, feedback, and/or inspiration they provided for this book, there are several colleagues I wish to thank. First, Cheryl Glenn, Andrea Lunsford, Susan Jarratt, and Bonnie Kyburz for their suggestions regarding the book's title. I am similarly indebted to Beth McClaren (UNLV) for her expert editing of the manuscript, for her willingness to field-test the book in her English 102 course, as well as for the feedback of her students. The library staff at UNLV, and particularly Priscilla Finley, also deserve my sincere appreciation, especially for their assistance on Chapter Two (Research). I am significantly indebted to Professor John Clark (University of South Florida), not only for some of the methods and materials in Chapter Six (Editing), but for providing the original inspiration for this book, which I offer as a grateful tribute to his memory. I would also like to thank my colleagues in the English Department, and particularly in the Writing and Rhetoric Program (Professors Jablonski, Tillery, Nagelhout, and Staggers) for their constant encouragement of my scholarly pursuits. I am especially grateful to my Department Chair, Chris Hudgins, for providing the writing and research time that enabled me to work on this book, while fulfilling my responsibilities as a WPA. I would also like to thank my erstwhile co-administrators in the First-Year Writing Program, Ruby Fowler, Carol Conder, and Elaine Bunker for their useful feedback on portions of this book, for their willingness to field-test portions of it in the Graduate Practicum (Eng 791) and in select English 102 sections, and more generally for their commitment to first-year writing and for the mutually supportive atmosphere they help foster. Deserving of my thanks and appreciation, as well, for their untiring assistance and support are my administrative collaborators in the English Department and in the Program in Writing and Rhetoric, Susan Summers, Michele Sanders, Allison Bredlau, Sylvia Blazo, and Tony Patricia. Perhaps most deserving of all of my deepest gratitude are the writing/composition teachers whom I have been fortunate enough to learn from over the years, including Norman Dessler (Acalanes High School/Lafayett, California.), Professor Gary Olson (Illinois State University), and Professor Joe Moxley (University of South Florida). Additionally, I would like to thank my colleagues at Fountainhead Press for their guidance and professionalism throughout this process: Felix Frazier, Scott Timian, Tim French, Shelley Smith, and Pat Bracken. I am, additionally, deeply humbled by the commitment and sacrifice of my parents, Joan and Harry Brown, in providing for my university education, for which I will remain forever grateful. Finally, a special word of thanks for she who is a constant source of light in my life, Shellmarie.

TABLE OF CONTENTS

PREFACE
Why Write?.. *xii*

CHAPTER 1
At Play in the Fields of the Word:
Strategies of Invention *1*

CHAPTER 2
"And I Quote":
Researching the Researchable Thesis..................................... *43*

CHAPTER 3
The Introduction: Rhetorical Strategies
& the First Moment of the Product *105*

CHAPTER 4
Depth Analysis &
the Second Moment of Persuasion *129*

CHAPTER 5
Climactic Assessment &
the Final Moment of Persuasion *165*

CHAPTER 6
Get it Write:
Editing in the Writing Workshop *175*

WORKS CITED *187*

Preface

Why Write?

The rhetorical strategies set forth in this field guide to academic writing are the byproduct of a thirty-year career devoted to academic writing and the teaching of it: lessons which, if learned, will help you, the student writer, meet with success not only in the marketplace of ideas that is the university, but in the marketplace of careers beyond it. The lessons are simple, learnable, and once grasped will give you a strategic advantage in the areas of oral and written communication, insofar as they comprise a source not only of personal empowerment, but of professional literacy across many disciplines.

I mention the career marketplace beyond the university for good reason. I speak with many employers—and they all tell me the same thing: "We are looking for two things in our prospective college graduates: strong communication skills (oral and written) and solid computer skills." This is a "killer" combination with which to enter the career marketplace: one that gives the effective communicator a strategic advantage over other job-seekers, who may have superior knowledge in a specialized field, but who lack either the written or interpersonal skills to communicate it effectively.

A case in point: Recently I had dinner with the Director of Admission/College of Medicine at a major university, who caught my attention with the following remark: "Guess where we're recruiting our doctors and nurses from? English majors!" I was taken aback. I could understand MBA programs and law schools recruiting heavily from English majors, given the emphasis on communication skills in those fields—but, schools of medicine? "Absolutely," he continued. "We can teach our doctors and nurses everything they need to know about medicine once we get them into our program, but what we really need are doctors and nurses who can *communicate effectively*: to each other, to their patients, to their next of kin, to insurance companies, etc., etc." This conversation drove home the relevancy, if not the centrality, of solid oral and written communication skills in today's marketplace.

Writing in the Margins is a practical guide to academic writing designed to foster success not only in your academic careers, but in your post-graduate, professional careers. If you think the art of persuasion and persuasive writing is irrelevant to your life or career goals, then I would ask you to consider the following:

- Tell the salesperson, who depends for his or her living on the ability to persuade you to buy a given product, that the art of persuasion is irrelevant to his or her success;
- Tell this to the politician running for office, or to the environmental lobbyist trying to persuade the politician to adopt a piece of legislation;
- Tell the advertising copywriter or the newspaper editorialist that the ability to persuade is not fundamental to his or her livelihood;
- Tell this to the citizen appearing before a judge in a small claims court;
- Tell the lawyer, who has to convince a jury that a defendant is guilty or innocent, that the ability to persuade is not essential to his or her success;
- Tell the doctor fighting a mal-practice suit, or trying to convince a patient to make life saving changes to his or her diet, or arguing for or against euthanasia, that the ability to persuade is irrelevant to his or her practice;
- Tell any employee seeking a raise or better benefits that the ability to speak persuasively is not in his or her interest;
- Finally, tell the job-seeker sitting in the interview room that the ability to convince an employer to hire him or her over another highly qualified applicant that the art of persuasion is not critical to his or her interest.

In fact, I would argue that persuasive communication practices pervade our culture, and particularly the career marketplace. *Writing in the Margins* is designed to hone your communication skills (oral and written), so that you may have a reasonable expectation of meeting with a high degree of success not only in your other courses, but in the career marketplace beyond.

The interactive approach to learning that is fundamental to your writing courses, and that is reinforced in *Writing in the Margins*, will help hone your oral communication skills. Further, the applicable, hands-on, nature of the following rhetorical strategies will enhance your ability to write with focus and concrete development, with emphasis and clarity across disciplines. If to these rhetorical strategies, you bring a willingness to learn and a faith in the outcome—if you are willing, as Peter Elbow advises, to play the "believing game" (with respect to yourself, these strategies, and your writing), then the prospects for your success as an academic writer become bright indeed. In return for this commitment to academic writing, you can expect to gain many practical benefits from the rhetorical strategies modeled in *Writing in the Margins*: the ability to assimilate a large quantity of data; to arrange it in an effective form; to give its parts the requisite emphasis, and the whole the desired level of correctness; to effectively introduce, succinctly state, concretely develop, and emphatically assess a significant and researchable thesis; and finally, to locate, assess, and effectively communicate information gathered from diverse sources. All are abilities that privilege success both academically and professionally. This is a sizable return on your investment.

This leads to an important question: is preparation for a career the only purpose of a higher education? Certainly not. However, given the cost of higher education, is it too much to expect that there should be some practical return on that investment? I think not. Nevertheless, I would argue this isn't the only reason, nor even the most important reason, for pursuing a higher education. Even if you never earn a single dollar from a college education, the experience is its own reward—and by that I mean, the pursuit of knowledge for its own sake (and the personal, even transformative enrichment associated with it). This sense of personal enrichment and/or empowerment is justification enough for a higher education.

However, there is yet a third, even loftier, justification for a college education beyond the practical rewards or personal enrichment associated with it. This has to do with fostering a sense of participatory citizenship through informed engagement, and with using education for the public good: to help solve the problems that we, as a society, face. It has to do with yoking higher education not just to the professional and the personal, but to the social. The rhetorical strategies in *Writing in the Margins* are designed to fulfill all three goals of a higher education. Thus, the university is not just a training ground for the career marketplace, nor a mere sanctuary for the pursuit of knowledge for its own sake, but an incubator for the informed citizenry upon which participatory democracy depends. Knowledge should be put to beneficial use—should serve not just the professional and personal interests of the individual, but the greater good of humankind. The oral and written literacy that *Writing in the Margins* is designed to foster will hopefully serve as a vital preamble to a rejuvenated sense of public intellectualism in the democratic marketplace of ideas: one that mingles the personal, the professional, and the public Self.

Get it Write.

> Sincerely,
>
> Stephen G. Brown, Director
> First-Year Program in Writing & Rhetoric
> University of Nevada, Las Vegas

Chapter One

At Play in the Fields of the Word: Strategies of Invention

"Invention is perhaps the most difficult part of rhetoric to teach."

—Sharon Crowley, 231

"Invention (in-ven-chen). A creation of the imagination . . . or process originated after study and experiment."

—Webster's Dictionary

Preview: Invention Strategies

- Collaborative strategies
- Webbing
- Free-Writing
- Writing-in-the-Margins
- Reader-Response Journal

The paradox of academic writing (and the teaching of it) is that we use a recursive process to achieve a linear product: one that will be read from left to right, top to bottom, and beginning to end. If the end product is linear, the process by which it is reached is circular, insofar as the writer keeps circling back to what has been written, as if plowing new material into a garden, pruning here and "growing" there (Elbow 12) until the desired effect of the writing on the reader is achieved. Consequently, the student must write (and the instructor must teach) to both the process and the product of academic writing. The trick is knowing when to write (and to teach) to each.

Writing in the Margins is, therefore, based on a fundamental assumption, reinforced by five decades of composition theory and practice, that although there are moments when both are occurring simultaneously (writing to the process and the product), generally an early emphasis on the process gradually shifts to a final emphasis on the product of academic writing: the thesis-driven, research-oriented paper. In other words, it is all a matter of timing, with respect to the emphasis that is given to process and product.

Therefore, writing strategies that are attuned to the recursive nature of the process in its beginning stages are more likely to achieve a balance between form and content, as opposed to those that privilege linearity throughout the teaching/writing process. This chapter (indeed this entire book) proceeds on the assumption that good writing (and writing pedagogy) foregrounds recursivity in the early phases and defers linearity to the latter stages of the process.

Everything in its own time.

That being said, the boundaries between these distinctions are fluid. As one moves from the beginning to the end of the writing process, a fundamental shift occurs from recursive to linear writing. That being said, the two often occur simultaneously in the middle phase of the process, where a mass of developed data begins to struggle to resolve itself into a linear form, in much the same way that a river damned by a mountain-slide must find a way through this interrupting mass. If the inventor dominates the early stages and the arranger the middle phase of the writing process, then the editor prevails toward journey's end. The academic writer must write effectively in all three modes (inventor, arranger, editor), which means developing effective strategies for each phase of this process, from free-writing and climactic arrangement to editing for clarity and correctness.

The purpose then of this text is to help the student-writer develop effective strategies during each of these "moments" of writing the academic paper. It is hoped that if the student absorbs the practical strategies of this "field guide to academic writing," that he or she will possess a useful rhetorical "tool bag" that can be used not only in the first-year writing sequence, but throughout the student's academic career, in courses across disciplines that emphasize the thesis-driven, evidence-based, research-oriented paper.

Writing in the Margins is also grounded in the assumption that these abilities (to write for focus, concreteness, and clarity; to introduce, state, develop, and assess a thesis) have very real "capital" beyond higher education, in the marketplace of professions, many of which increasingly privilege the kinds of written communication skills this book emphasizes. The student can, therefore, expect a "good return" on his or her investment in *Writing in the Margins,* insofar as proficiency in the strategies it emphasizes favors success not only in college course work, but in the professional work-place beyond.

As *Webster's* definition suggests, academic writing (at least at its most effective) draws on both the recursive and the linear processes of writing, draws on both the analytical and the imaginative faculties of the human mind, invites the writer to write from both sides of the brain, as it were: not only from the analytical left side, but from the creative right side. This is a good thing, for it makes for more balanced writing, in which a focus is developed not only with the concrete substance of the left side of the brain (logic, quotes, facts, etc.), but also with the colorful inventions of the right side as well (figurative language, metaphors, alliterations, AND those rich avenues of concrete development DISCOVERED during the invention phase of the process, with which the writing of an academic paper begins).

It is no coincidence that lawyers refer to the initial phases of building an argumentative case as the DISCOVERY PHASE, for this is when their case is literally discovered, through investigation of the relevant precedents, development of the evidence, and discovery of the relevant "points and authorities" with which they will build their case. It is during this phase that the academic writer similarly INVENTS his or her argument: by discovering all the available means of developing it, selecting the most effective of those means, and hypothesizing a tentative arrangement for them: one that is not fixed in stone, but flexible enough to change in accordance with the subsequent development of what has been discovered during the INVENTION phase.

The scientific works of some of the greatest minds (Darwin, Freud, Nietzsche, Carson) have endured not only because of their scientific value, but because of their literary merit as well. Each made effective use not only of the scientific method, but of figurative language to make clear their complex meanings. They wrote, in other words, from the left as well as from the right side of their brains, enlivening the critical with the figurative, informing the analytical with the creative. In short, these thinkers were not only great scientists, but effective writers—which makes their science accessible to the layman even today.

Yet, far too often, the inventive, the colorful, the creative is taught as if it has no place in the academic essay, as if it should be confined to the creative writing workshop. Many students are taught, in effect, to leave their imaginations at the door. Though imaginative writing in an academic paper may be tolerated, little emphasis is given to it in the classroom, little time and less practice is devoted to developing this critical faculty in the academic writing process. This emphasis on the analytical to the exclusion of the inventive is problematic, for it undermines the persuasive effects of an essay by compromising reader interest and often by precluding imaginative depth analysis. My point here is that the path to rich, analytical development of a researchable focus often lies through the imagination—if it does not, indeed, commence there.

Writing in the Margins begins with this chapter on Invention because of a simple assumption: if my experience as an academic writer has shown me anything, it is that a good paper begins with an imaginative search for avenues of development, then proceeds to concrete development of those discovered avenues (or criteria) of analysis. In other words, what ends up as the product of the left brain begins with the activity of the right. Every inventive or recursive activity of the process has but a single aim: to enrich the content and heighten the effect of the final product.

Writing in the Margins is predicated on yet a final assumption: that writing, not thinking, first is the best activity for developing a paper's focus. In other words, instead of thinking before you write, you should write before you think—in order to discover what you think. The fundamental assumption here is that thought comes, not before, but after language (writing): that the threshold to the deeper realms of thought lies through writing. In other words, it isn't until you pick up the pen and begin to write (or until you put fingers to keypad) that ideas start to occur, which otherwise would have remained inaccessible. This is the most useful lesson to be learned from this chapter, and the greatest wisdom to be gleaned from this book.

Believe in it and practice it—and your academic writing will take on that depth of engagement, that nuance of analysis, that density of development that are the hallmarks of all effective persuasive discourse. Writing in this mode may be messy and excessive. Nevertheless, in order to get to the point where you can say 20 words in 10, you must first allow yourself the freedom to say 10 words in twice that number. You have to risk writing nothing of any worth to *discover* anything worthy of being written—the key word here being "discover."

The first strategy of academic writing is, therefore, simple: write to discover what you think. Let the pen (or your fingers on the keypad) wander at will through the unknown landscape of the subject at hand. I call this phase of the discovery process "At Play in the Fields of the Word."

If you want your writing to reflect Play of Mind (another essential virtue of all effective academic writing), you first have to let your mind play with language: like a batter taking practice swings in order to hit one out of the park. Language is the field of play for the mind to sport upon. A good academic paper is nothing more (nor less) than the product of the union between mind and language, thought and word. The sequential relationship between word and thought is something like the central wisdom expressed in the film *A Field of Dreams*: "If you build it, they will come." If you write, you will think. If you start playing with words on a page (or a screen), ideas will come to you, that never would have occurred otherwise. This phenomenon has occurred so often in my own academic writing career that I no longer even question its credibility. I write not with the wish, but the certainty that this will happen. Thought happens—when you write. Ideas need ink to be born.

I start out producing far more words than I need, or will have room for in a paper. Consequently, what will end as a ten page paper often begins as a forty page Frankenstein of roughly organized material. Somewhere, however, in that roughly blocked-out draft is my ten-page paper. The process can be messy, time consuming, and laborious—which is why enough time must be allowed for this process to work in your favor, whether you are working a 20-page draft into a 10-page final edit, or an 8-page rewrite into a 5-7page paper. If deferred until the 11th hour, this process will work against you. Consequently, I like to begin early; in fact, I commence writing a paper when I'm reading the sources about which I will write, whether primary or secondary: by keeping a reading-response journal and by writing-in-the-margins of another's text. But more on this in a moment.

As a result of this process, the words I do end up with prove worthy of their place in the "final cut." To find the right ones, you often have to write the wrong ones: another fundamental paradox of academic writing.

Perhaps the definition of "genius," when it comes to writing, is being able to write the "right" words "off the top of your head," without having to go through any process of revision or drafting to "get it right." Shakespeare, apparently, was such a writer, given the testimony of his contemporaries, including his "friend and rival, Ben Jonson [who] wrote, 'that in his writing, whatsoever he penned, he never blotted out a line'" (qtd. in Greenblatt, 189). So too, apparently, was Mozart, who composed sublimely finished music the first moment he touched pen to paper, as if merely "taking dictation" from his mind. This is because artists like this do most, if not all, of their composing in their minds, so that when it comes time to put pen to paper they are in effect merely "taking dictation" from their muses. Most of us, however, do not "get it right" the first time. We need to work it and rework it. Consequently, a strong work ethic is a good thing to possess (or to develop) when writing an academic paper—work that involves a good deal of "play" when it comes to our working relationship with language.

Obviously, what we're trying to cultivate here is a certain attitude toward writing, and the writing process in particular—a certain "consciousness" that is grounded in basic assumptions, that privileges specific practices, and that fosters confidence in the result—in which a circular process is used to reach a linear product.

You have to work to find the "right" words. Diamonds like to hide in the rough. If you're willing to go into the "rough" areas of your thought, you may find the diamonds you're seeking, that drew you there. But before you can "cut," "finish," and "mount" them, you must first "find" them. You must go into the field in search of them—and in this case, the field is the empty page or the deserted screen.

This chapter models various rhetorical strategies of invention and discovery, designed to enrich the content and heighten the effect of a persuasive essay, by discovering the most effective means of developing its focus, and by positing a tentative arrangement of that development. Having decided on a focus for the persuasive paper or personal essay, the immediate challenge is to discover the most effective means of developing that focus—again, the operative word being "discover." Having tentatively settled on the focus of your argumentative paper (that is, on a researchable thesis or opinion), how do you go about effectively developing it?

Many students often list "getting started" as the hardest part of writing a paper. The rhetorical strategies in this chapter are designed to overcome this problem of intellectual inertia often encountered at the very outset of the persuasive journey. Whether you use "webbing," clustering" or "incubating," brain-storming, free-writing, outlining or "more complex modern systems of invention [that] include Stephen Toulmin's claim/warrant/data model [or a model] derived from Kenneth Burke's 'pentad' of motives," (Crowley 232), each of these strategies has proven effective for putting the writer "into the moment" of the subject matter, for getting beneath the surface to the real "meat of the matter," for getting beyond the clichés to the "deeper grammar" of an issue: for quickly discovering fruitful avenues of development, categories of inquiry, sub-heads of analysis and argument. Though each of these techniques has its uses, I am going to model an invention strategy that has received less attention in the classroom, though it is ideally suited, theoretically and practically, to the interactive, student-centered classroom.

I. Collaborative Invention Strategies: The Group-as-Writer

Thesis and Criteria of Development:

This section is designed to give the student hands-on practice devising a central research question, crafting a working thesis that answers this question, then discovering substantive ways to develop that focus. The strategies are based on the assumption that "two (or more) heads are better than one," which is based on a further assumption: that knowledge is constructed socially, through language. Hence, the relevance of this invention activity to the student-centered, interactive classroom. It is a variation of a strategy first modeled by Toby Fulwiler, a pioneering advocate of writing across the curriculum.

Activity 1: Research Questions

Time Frame: Portion of class period (with follow-up activities).
- In a small collaborative group (3-4 students), assign the roles of

a "recorder" to write down the group's findings, and a "reporter" to report those findings to the class. Remaining members of the group play the role of "facilitators," generating ideas, keeping the group on task, etc.
- As a group, "brainstorm" practice topics for a paper. These can be serious or playful. The "recorder" makes a list of these topics, as follows:

hand guns	organ donors
Barbie	front porch
global warming	tattooing and body piercing
life of a first-year student	rap music and lyrics

- In collaboration with peers, each student drafts a *central research question* related to their chosen topic, in journal.
- Each member of the group free-writes on a topic of their choice in journal.
- Share free-write with group.
- "Reporters" share one topic and its central research question with the class, as follows.

  Should private ownership of hand guns be abolished?

  What are the causes and effects of acrid rain?

  Does Barbie reinforce negative female stereotypes?

  Should Gangsta' rap lyrics be censored for their violent, misogynistic, or racist contents?

  What is the significance of the front porch in suburban and rural America?

Activity 2: Criteria
- In journals, record the criteria you would use to develop your specific topic. Be inclusive; think of as many criteria for developing your topic as possible.
- Share your criteria with the group.

- Other members of group provide overlooked criteria.
- The "recorder" compiles a list of criteria for each topic, as follows:

Topic: The Front Porch

Development
1. uses (hammock, rocker, bird feeder, sun bathing, reading)
2. sensory details (sights, sounds, smells)
3. types (screen, redwood deck, wrap around)
4. history
5. subjective response (moods, emotions, upset, calming)
6. porch at various times of day
7. porch in various seasons of year
8. porch in various weather conditions
9. under the porch (hide'n seek, sexual rites of passage, gothic treatment/horror, the dog's napping spot)

- "Reporter" selects one of the topics and shares its list of criteria with the class.

Follow-up: Free-write
- The group selects one of the topics for practice writing. Each member of the group chooses one of the "criteria of development" and free-writes on it in journal.
- Share free-writes with group.
- "Reporter" shares one with class, reading aloud.

Activity 3: Fulwiler's "Radical Limitation" of Focus
- Each group member selects what he or she considers to be the 3–4 most effective criteria for developing the topic of choice, and lists in journal.
- Share list of criteria with group.

- Group negotiates the final list of criteria for each topic.
- The "recorder" compiles a master list.
- The "reporter" selects a topic and its limited list of criteria to share with class.

Activity t4: Arrangement
- Arrange the 3-4 criteria of development for your topic in reverse order of effectiveness, beginning with weakest (#4) and proceeding to the strongest (#1).
- Share this arrangement with the group.
- The group negotiates a final tentative ranking of development criteria.
- The "reporter" shares the final arrangement rankings with the class, as follows:

Topic/Focus: The Front Porch and the Rural Sublime

Development:
1. sensory details (sights, sounds, smells): present tense/hook
2. history/designs: background/context
3. memories: past tense-to-climax
4. hours of day
5. seasons
6. weather
7. under the porch (hide'n seek, a lost cat, sexual adventures, a lonely day locked out in the rain)
8. conclusion: retrospective assessment; back to present tense; clincher/end quote

Activity 5: Follow up/Free-Write
- At home, free-write a response to each criteria of development.
- Share in group.

Writing-to-Learn: Paper

- Formulate a central research question on paper topic, and record it in journal.
- Draft a thesis statement that answers this question, that succinctly and forcefully tells *what* you will argue.
- Add a sentence or two, listing the criteria by which this thesis will be developed—that tells *how* you will develop your argument (thesis).
- Share question, thesis, and criteria of development in group.

Activity 6: Follow-Ups/ Revisions

The Extended Free-Write

- At home, in journal, free-write on each criterion-for-developing your thesis. The purpose of these free-writes is to discover your thoughts regarding the subject, further avenues of development, and other useful tangents you might have passed over in your first hastily written free-write. Take these new tacks and follow where they lead. When one runs out, return to your point of departure and resume on your original heading. If you've ever heard of the wilderness sport of "orienteering," free-writing is similar, insofar as you are following up "leads" in order to develop as many as possible, while better orienting yourself to your focus. The other useful analogy here is that of the investigative journalist or the lawyer, discovering as many "leads" as possible to develop his or her "story" or "case."
- Bring these extended free-writes to class and share in group, soliciting any "leads" that might have been overlooked.
- Underline your favorite sentence, or the one that best captures the focus of the entire free-write, or that announces a useful lead.
- At home, type up a mini-draft of one of these categories of development (1-2 pages) and share in group.
- At home, incorporate any useful feedback, re-type, and hand-in for grade.

Focus and Development

A common mistake first-year writers make in their early drafts is trying to cover everything under the sun about their topic. The result is often writing that skims generically along the surface of the subject without ever engaging its "deeper grammar." The writing lacks substance or depth, suffers from a lack of focus and concrete development of that focus—perhaps the two most essential ingredients of effective academic writing. Focus and development. Students tend to take a "shot-gun" approach to a topic, spraying words onto the page in a random order. While this may be good for getting started or untracked, it is counter-productive if it isn't adjusted for focus and depth of development. What is needed isn't a shotgun, but a trowel—or some other instrument for digging. How to get students into the depths of a given topic is one of the biggest challenges facing teachers. Similarly, how to get yourself-as-writer into the depths of a topic is one of the most immediate challenges facing the student.

Fulwiler's "Radical Limitation" of Focus

- At home, rewrite your free-write, following Fulwiler's guidelines for "radically limiting" the focus of the paper. In other words, write the same amount on a limited focus. Instead of writing 2-3 pages on a favorite season, write 2-3 pages on an hour in an October forest. Instead of writing 2-3 pages on your childhood neighborhood, write 2-3 p on the neighborhood bully, a childhood pal, a favorite pet, a special place, etc.

Example 1
1. 1st draft: "Two months working at McDonald's"
2. 2nd draft: "One day in July" or "The worst day on the job"

Example 2
1. "Summer on my granpa's farm"
2. "A romantic hour in the cornfield"

Limiting the scope of your focus adds concrete development to it—

one of the hallmarks of effective academic writing. It adds *density and/or depth* to the content: a virtue to be sought first, always, and forever. Moreover, by writing "more about less" in this fashion you are simplifying your task as a writer. For now, instead of needing ten "incidents" to develop a broad focus, you only need a few to develop your "radically limited" focus. This strategy pays huge and immediate dividends when writing papers that require *close textual analysis* where instead of responding to a dozen quotes superficially, you are able to develop the significance of two or thee in *depth and at length.*

- Share these "radically limited" free-writes in group.
- Underline your favorite sentence, or sentence that best announces the free-write's focus.
- Share aloud in group.
- Volunteers share entire free-write and selected sentences with class.

Free-Write: The Fresh Angle

Another means of adding substance to your focus is to free-write on it from a fresh perspective. For example, if writing a critical assessment of Barbie's significance in contemporary American culture, you might further develop your view from one of several perspectives, as follows:

- from a personal perspective
- from memory
- from a sensory-detail description of her
- from the perspective of an adolescent or pre-adolescent girl
- from the perspective of a mother
- from the perspective of a toy manufacturer or sales rep
- from a feminist perspective
- from a male, sexual perspective
- from the opposite (pro vs con) perspective to your own point of view

- from Barbie's perspective (or Ken's)

Writing-to-Learn: The Fresh Angle

At home, add on to your "radically limited" free-write, by writing from a "fresh angle," as follows:
- By writing in an *objective*-only mode, recording objective details.
- By writing from *memory* only.
- By writing from *sensory details*.
- By writing from the *opposite point of view*.
- By assuming the *role* of a particular person, and writing from that perspective.
- By assuming the *role* of the teacher, and writing self-reflexively about your own writing.
- By writing from a *subjective perspective*, from a purely emotional response.
- Share this rewritten free-write in group.
- Underline favorite sentence or sentence that best expresses the focus of the free-write.
- Volunteers share aloud with class.
- Type up a mini-draft of your free-writes, cobbling together your "radically limited" free-write and your "fresh angle free-write."
- Share in group.
- Incorporate useful feedback, type up, and hand in for grade.

This kind of writing (and thinking) outside the box of an original focus adds freshness, depth, and density to the writing. By switching from present to past, from sensory detail to memory, from an objective to a subjective perspective, from a "pro" to "con" point of view, from logic to passion, you may discover a fresh means of developing your focus. And while some of what is written may ultimately prove irrelevant or of no use, some may indeed provide fresh concrete development of the limited focus.

Conclusion/Summary

The invention/discovery/revision process is a circular (recursive) activity, in which the same ground is returned to and reworked for focus and substance, depth and development, using the following writing-to-learn sequence::

- Initial free-writes (lst draft)
- At-home add-on (amplify and pick up missed "leads;") (lst draft)
- "Radical Limitation" of focus (2nd draft)
- The "Fresh Angle" (3rd draft)
- Group feedback (3rd draft)
- Typed, edited draft (4th draft)
- Group feedback (editing workshop)
- Final typed mini-paper

In this manner, a limited focus is concretely developed through free-writing revisions, peer-feedback groups, and individual conferences with the instructor, as part of a writing intensive, developmental process that uses discovery and invention as a path to substantive development of a significant, yet limited focus. Further, since making a claim (argumentative focus) and supporting it with evidence is every discipline's goal in writing, these classroom practices are applicable across the curriculum, throughout the student's academic career. If mastered, they have great currency in the career marketplace, as well. Collaborative invention strategies can also be a fun, lively introduction to academic writing, helping to break the ice, establish the "workshop" approach and generate a sense of community-as-writers early on in the process.

II. Webbing as Invention

Another simple, yet effective invention strategy, especially for visual learners, is Clustering or Webbing. This is a quick and easy way to get immediately from a thesis into its most useful and immediate criteria of development. In the center of a blank page, simply write your focus in one word, then draw a circle around it. Radiating outward from this central focus, draw a series of spokes or lines: one for each criteria of development you discover, written in a one-word caption at the end of each spoke. Let's assume, for the sake of instruction, our topic was the focus of this chapter: Invention Strategies. The corresponding web might look something like this:

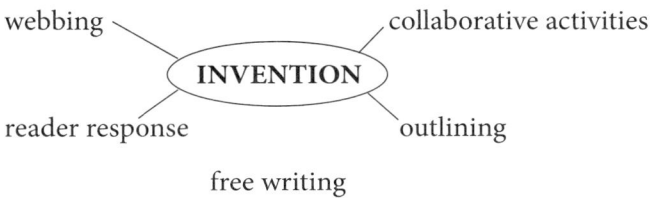

Let's take another example:

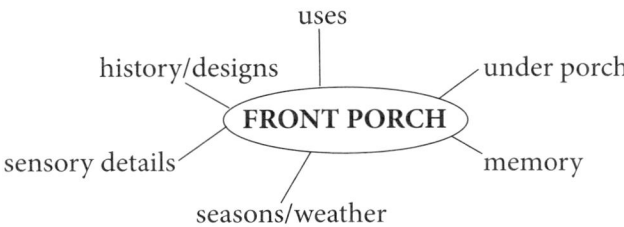

Each of these criteria of development can, of course, be further sub-divided on the page, to reflect the sub-headings of development within a given category. The important thing to remember is that a WEB, like the lists generated by the collaborative groups, is not a master blueprint to be rigidly adhered to in the generation of your paper, but merely a means of jump-starting your engagement with the topic: a point of entry into the detailed depths of any given topic, as well as the beginnings of an effective arrangement pattern for the various "points and authorities" with which you will develop the topic (focus). These invention strategies should not be viewed as "plans" that are "set in stone," to be religiously implemented, but as maps that lead quickly and directly to a deeper engagement with the topic, which once engaged must be given its own head, as inspiration and further discovery dictates. Many an effective thought only appears after writing has begun. An essay planned in detail, and written according to the dictates of this plan, precludes the serendipitous emergence of thoughts and aborts the very "play of mind" that is the essence of effective academic writing and the one quality for which every reader yearns.

- Share your web in group, soliciting additional criteria.
- "Reporter" compiles master list of "webs."
- "Recorder" selects one to share with class.

Writing to Learn: Mini-Paper

- At home in journal, follow same process, free-writing on a particular criterion of development.
- Share in group.
- Add-on at home, amplifying the free-write and picking up any over-looked leads.
- Share in groups.
- At home, free-write by "radically limiting" the focus.
- Share in group.
- At home, free-write from a "fresh angle."
- Edit for clarity and correctness, type up mini-draft (1-2 pages).
- Share in group (editing workshop).
- Free-write additional criteria of development, following same process for each criterion.
- Type up final edited draft of mini paper (2-3 pages) or paper (5-7 pages) and hand in.

III. Free-Writing as Invention

We have been talking a lot about "free-writing." In this section I want to focus in greater detail on this invention strategy, for it is one of the most practical means of discovering useful avenues for developing a focus (thesis). Free-writing enables the student writer to plunge head-first into a given topic. It puts the writer immediately into the "moment" of writing. Peter Elbow, who pioneered this mode of invention, provides a succinct rationale for it:

> I had to write down without stopping whatever came to me in my thinking about my general topic, and above all I had to stop worrying about whether what I was writing at the moment was any good. I had to invite chaos and bad writing. Then, after I had written a lot and figured out a lot of thinking, I could go back over and reassert control and try and make it good. (xviii)

This section models various rhetorical strategies related to free-writing, by introducing the student to 12 kinds of "free-writes" designed to improve academic writing, each an important strategy to add to your academic writing "tool kit," as follows:

1. The *impromptu* free-write, to discover what you think regarding a given issue, the first "swing" you take at an issue, usually your first response to the central research question.

2. The *add-on* free-write, in which you simply re-read what you wrote, pick up where you left off, and add on to it.

3. The *missed lead* free-write, in which you re-read the "impromptu" and "add on" free-writes, searching for those "leads" that were there, but which were overlooked in your initial haste to record your thoughts on the subject. The relationship of writing to thought is such that our thoughts always run ahead of our pen. This "missed lead" free-write is intended to recuperate those useful ideas which may have crossed our mind but which eluded our pen. Free-writing is somewhat like a "grab-fest" in which you try to grab every idea as it occurs—in vain. A second pass through the subject is as necessary as it is rewarding, for during it you often succeed in capturing a little more rhetorical "lightning in a bottle." Often, these "missed leads" turn out to be some of the best leads.

4. The *radical limitation* free-write, in which you write the same amount on a radically limited focus.
5. The *fresh angle* free-write, in which you free-write on the topic from a fresh perspective—writing from memory, or from a personal perspective, etc.
6. A variation of this is the *flip-the-script* free-write, in which you write from the opposite point of view.
7. Another variation is the *role-playing* free-write, in which you adopt the perspective of a person likely to have an opinion on the issue at hand.
8. Another variation is the *personal* free-write, in which you write from a purely subjective point of view, tying your personal experience into the issue.
9. The *reader-response* free-write, in which you respond to a quote from a reading or field interview.
10. The *rebuttal* free-write, in which you respond to the counter-arguments, or to the counter-argument that sparks the greatest reaction.
11. The *peroration* free-write, in which you end your argument with a strong personal statement.
12. The *climactic assessment* free-write, in which you end your argument by retrospectively assessing its significance, its implications for the future, by answering the "so what; why is this so important?"

As you can readily see, there are free-writes for every moment of the argumentative paper, for the introduction (#1, 8), the body (# 2-7, 9, 10), and the conclusion (#11, 12). By free-writing at every moment of the argumentative journey, the student increases the likelihood that his or her writing will possess the two most desired virtues of academic writing: voice and substance. In the remainder of this section, I show what these free-writing strategies look like in action.

Activity 1: Free-write

- Devise a central research question for your topic, and record in journal.

  Example 1: Should private ownership of guns be banned? All guns? Just hand guns? Just semi-automatic weapons?

  Example 2: Should sports teams with names or mascots that demean Native Americans change them?

- In journals, free-write a response to the central research question.
- Share in group.
- At home, add-on to the initial free-write.
- Then re-read what you have written, pursuing any "leads" overlooked in these initial free-writes.
- Share in group.

Student samples

Example 1. Pro ban: "Assault weapons should be banned to the general public. Private ownership of all other types of guns should be highly regulated. Regulations should include, classes, training, awareness, and last, testing. Testing knowledge of guns, proper use, and appropriate behavior when around guns. Having grown up in Idaho, I know many would object to this. However, every newscast tells of another senseless act of taking an innocent life."

Example 2. Con ban: "I do not think private ownership of guns should be banned. As Americans, we have certain rights, and this is one of them. I do, think, however, we should have stricter laws. Regarding ownership of guns. These should include stricter punishments for laws broken. Also, I think we need to make it less accessible for the wrong people to obtain access to guns. Parents need to do more to protect their children. I think if we have more education regarding gun control and if TV & movies stop glamorizing the use of it, it would make it safer."

- In group, re-read, underlining favorite sentence.
- Volunteers share aloud with class.

A Writing-to-Learn Sequence: Follow Up/a Fresh Angle

- At home, in journal, free-write on the issue of gun control or Native American mascots from a personal perspective, using examples drawing on any relevant experience you've had with the issue at hand. If writing on the "mascot" issue, write about a time when you felt discriminated against, whether because of your ancestry, religion, gender, social class—or some other factor that marked you as "different," that reinforced your sense of "exclusion," or in some other way, approach the issue from a personal, subjective perspective.
- "Flip-the-Script:" At home free-write on the issue from the opposite point of view.
- "Play a Role:" Free-write on the gun issue from the point of view of a gunshot victim, relative of a gunshot victim, a gun owner, gun manufacturer, NRA lobbyist, anti-gun or pro gun congressman, hunter, criminal, prison inmate, etc.
- If writing on the "mascot" issue, free-write from the point of view of a Native American, a sports fan, a high school/college student, a person whose ethnic heritage has similarly been impugned by stereotypic images, names, etc.
- Share in group.
- Underline sentence that most succinctly states your view or represents your writing at its best.

Group Work: Thesis and Criteria of Development Workshop

- In journal, write your answer to the central research question in the most succinct and forceful language you can. Then generate a comprehensive list of criteria for developing this thesis.
- Share thesis and criteria of development in group. Responders suggest ways to strengthen the thesis, by making it more emphatic and/or scholarly in tone: by using a more dramatic verb,

by front-loading the verb, by selectively upgrading the diction, etc. Responders also suggest ways to strengthen the criteria of development, first by noting any useful criteria that have been overlooked, then by reaching a consensus on the 2 or 3 most useful criteria of development, and finally by negotiating a ranking of the criteria, weakest to strongest.
- At home, incorporate these suggestions into a revised and upgraded thesis, as well as a sentence listing the criteria by which it will be developed.

Field Work
- In journal, interview people, taking notes on their responses to the aforementioned central research question.
- Share in group.
- Share your favorite quote, one you might use in a paper.

Activity 2: Mini-Paper
- Using as sources your free-writes, field interviews, and any readings related to the issue, type a draft of a mini-paper (2-3 pages), in which you succinctly and forcefully state your position, announce your criteria for developing it, and provide a couple pages of concrete development.

Group Work: Focus, Development, and Arrangement Workshop

Share draft of mini-paper in group. Group responders highlight those passages that come alive or generate the most interest, providing facilitative feedback on the paper's strengths. A second round of responses is generated pertaining to the paper's problematic passages, which are similarly conveyed to the writer. This constructive feedback ignores the surface-level problems for the moment, focusing on the "deeper rhetorical grammar" of the writing (focus, development, organization/arrangement, and clarity, etc.), noting, as follows:
- additional ways to develop the writer's point of view.

- ways to improve its organization or arrangement, cut and paste suggestions.
- passages that need to be edited for clarity, where the meaning got obscured or lost in the wording.
- sentences or passages to delete.

Conclusion/Summary

By putting yourself immediately and continuously into the "moment" of writing by free-writing in response to the central research question, in response to quotes from the readings or field interviews, and in response to the counter-arguments, you are more likely to produce writing as lively as it is substantive, whose content is enlivened by a strong writerly voice, that is enriched by fresh perspectives and cogent criteria of development—by writing which, in its search for meaning, discovers the most fruitful "leads" to follow, which "leads" writer and reader as well into the depths of the issue or text at hand. Take these free-writing strategies then and make them a regular part of your rhetorical "tool kit" for writing the academic paper as follows:

- Impromptu free-writing to discover thought.
- An *add-on* free-write to further discover and develop your ideas and opinions.
- A *missed lead* free-write to discover and develop missed "leads".
- A *radical limitation* free-write, in which you write the same amount on a radically limited focus.
- A *fresh angle* free-write, in which you develop your position from a fresh perspective (memory vs. sensory detail; objective vs. subjective, etc).
- A *flip the script* free-write, in which you write from the opposite point of view.
- A *role-playing* free-write, in which you adopt the perspective of another "voice" in the debate.

- A *personal* free-write, in which you write from a personal point of view, tying your own experience into the topic/issue.
- A *reader-response* free-write, in which you respond to a quote from a reading or field interview.
- A *rebuttal* free-write, in which you refute the counter arguments.
- A *peroration* free-write, in which you make a strong personal statement.
- A *climactic assessment* free-write in which you develop the implications of your point of view (or the opposite point of view) answer the "so what?" or retrospectively assess the importance of your argument.

IV. Reader Response as Invention: Free-Writing in the Margins

> "No context can enclose writing, which constantly grafts itself to other chains of writing and signification."
> —Jasper Neel, 113

I would like, at this point, to model a free-writing strategy more effective than the previous strategies combined: writing in the margins. This strategy combines the acts of critical reading and critical writing. Further, it operates on a simple, yet fundamental assumption: that the most fecund site for discovering your own thoughts on a given topic is not the empty page (or computer screen) that awaits your free-writing pen or fingertips, but the empty margins of an Other's text. It is there, in proximity to an Other's words, that I start "talking back" to the text, selectively challenging its reasoning, questioning its assumptions, marking quotes or facts I want to appropriate for my own argument. It is a very predatory process. An invasion, if you will, of another's carefully staked out territory. A critical transgression. An interrogative incursion. A marginal cross-examination. If, as bell hooks asserts, the margins of a dominant culture are a strategic site for waging resistance to it, then similarly the margins of another's text are ideal sites for initiating "resistant" readings of it, for giving birth to your own critical "reading." In the "heat and light" of its words, your own are born.

Virtually every paper I write has its genesis in this white space encompassing an Other's words. These margins afford just enough space for my own text to grab hold of it, attach itself to it, like a parasite to a host. If you think this is problematic, recall that virtually every one of Shakespeare's plays began in just this fashion: arising from the words of an Other. As Stephen Greenblatt observes, "[t]hroughout Shakespeare's career as a playwright, he was a brilliant poacher—deftly entering into territory marked out by others, taking for himself what he wanted, and walking away with the prize under the keeper's nose" (152). The ideas of others are the favorite hunting grounds for Genius, for it takes this raw material and transmutes it into something entirely its own.

An academic paper evolves in the same manner, growing out of the earth of others' words. Reading begets writing: reading "between the lines" of an Other's text produces the lines of your own text. To put this another way: the lines of your own writing begin "between the lines" of another's, in the spaces between and around those words. The spaces between those words give your own "room to breathe."

Though the words of an Other's text give the illusion of continuity, they, in fact, exist amidst multiple discontinuities, which invite commentary, interpretation, "back talk" and dialogue. Some gaps in a text are wider than others: wide enough to "drive a truck" through them. Others may be so subtle that writing in them is like threading a needle's eye, stitching them with your own words, as if weaving into its threads your own interpretative pattern—or unraveling its own well-woven webs with the "hook" of your own needle. Indeed, writing in the margins and gaps of an Other's text is somewhat like using a crocheting needle to "hook" into a well woven fabric, "knitting" your own meanings amidst its own, sometimes unraveling its threads to "knit" your own interpretation from them.

Yet, to my knowledge, this is a very under-theorized and under-taught invention strategy, despite its effectiveness and applicability to the first-year composition class, and to the thesis-driven, research paper in particular. Simply stated, the act of critical writing begins with the act of critical reading. As most academic papers are assigned in the context of course readings, the acts of writing and reading are "joined at the hip," as it were. No text is created in the isolation chamber of its author's intellect; every text is, to some degree, a byproduct of other texts. Hence, the text of your writing is, to a very real degree, the offspring of the texts you read. For me, therefore, the act of writing begins with the act of reading—specifically, in the margins of the texts I'm reading.

It is there, in those narrow, white, and blank spaces that border a text that my paper begins its journey. A paper that ends as a freestanding, single-authored entity begins in the margins of another text, as a "supplement" to it, as a running commentary upon it. There, in those margins, I begin "talking back" to the text as I read. In effect, I am already writing my paper, trying out my ideas in response to those of the text I'm reading. A student essay begins as an "intervention" in another text, whose meaning it amplifies, amends, supplements, contradicts, and argues with. A paper begins by invading the margins of another text, which it "rewrites," perhaps responding to the things the original text has omitted (its "absences"), perhaps responding to its contradictions, perhaps adding a "yeah, but what about. . . ?"—or perhaps finding associations between the passage under consideration and previous or subsequent passages, noting rhetorical patterns, recursive images, or any number of features that collectively make up the text and that invite (and reward) analysis of it.

The point is, an academic paper begins by superimposing itself upon another text—in reality, upon a host of other texts. This other text is really a "pre-text" for your own. This is, indeed, good news, for it eliminates one of the most problematic aspects of writing the thesis-driven, research paper: getting started. The starting point has already been provided.

With pen in hand, you begin reading—and as you are reading, you are searching for evidence of those things about which you want to write (perhaps the author's use of figurative language, for example), or for those passages that spark a response, with which you strongly agree or disagree, or that raise questions in your mind, or that resonate with earlier or later passages, or with other texts. The point is, to start "dialoguing" or "conversing" with the text. You take over its margins, appropriate them as your own territory. With your words, you surround the words of the author, shouldering your way into his or her text, writing between the lines, in the spaces.

Moreover, any text (whether well or poorly written) will open spaces for "dialogue" with its readers, will invite this "exchange." The more complex a text, the more it opens itself to multiple readings, the less inclined it is to surrender its meanings easily, at first glance. Its words are like uncoupled boxcars, begging to be "coupled" to your own. Indeed, no text is complete until it has been grafted-onto by other texts. As Jasper Neel observes:

> An entire text or any part of a text remains forever liable to extraction from its current context... [T]exts and parts of texts find themselves grafted onto other texts and find that other texts graft onto them.... For a text to be read, a reader must extract it from the author's protection. (113-114)

You are in a sense midwife to the text's meanings. Meaning is the child of the intercourse between text and interpreter.

These "graftings," these inter-textual tidbits of marginalia, are the sproutings from which a paper grows, taking root in the shadows of another's words: by responding to what has been left out, or left unsaid; taking issue with an unstated, yet problematic assumption; noting a contradiction in the argument; a pattern in the imagery; strongly agreeing or disagreeing with a quote; registering a question (or a mere question mark).

Often, what I intend to be merely a one word response takes on a life of its own, creating a second text to that which I'm reading, wrapping around it in the margins, as I turn the book sideways, then upside down, sometimes spilling onto the next page. In fact, I am free-writing in the margins, discovering my thoughts to myself in response to another, brain-storming in ink beside the ink of an Other—in essence, giving birth to my first draft.

Respond, respond, respond. Reading, thus, is no mere passive absorption of another's text, but becomes an active and interactive "conversation" between two texts: the author's words and your own. Note: this strategy of writing-in-the-margins is not just part of the Invention phase, but also of the Research phase of your paper, inasmuch as responding to texts (and the words of others) is the essence of academic writing. Consequently, this strategy of writing-in-the-margins of texts is emphasized not just in chapter one, but in chapters two and three ("Research" and "Depth Analysis").

Writing in the Margins/The Process at Work

What does this marginal "back talk" look like in action?

The first step is to "graft" your words onto the text you are reading. While reading, if your eye is "glued" to the page, your ear is listening for your own "back talk"—and your pen is poised to give voice to this interrupting tongue of your intellect. Thus, never read without pen in hand. The acts of reading and writing literally go "hand in hand"—should occur concomitantly. They are "kissing cousins," if you will. For you are not only writing about reading, but writing while you are reading. Be vigilant, opportunistic, and predatory—and soon your pen will be filling the margins with your own text, which when transferred to your own territory, your own empty page, becomes more fully your own—though never entirely. The Other is always present in your words, though enclosed in quotations, paraphrases, and parenthetical page references. All the student needs to begin this "exchange" is a pen, and some space in the margins of the text where that pen can play with language. Not having a pen while reading is akin to showing up to a basketball court without a basketball.

Following are several examples from my own work, illustrative of this process. They model the twofold sequence of this invention strategy: writing in the margins, then free-writing on these individual grafts. Sometimes, these responses include nothing more than a series of checks beside an apt quote (✓✓✓, ✓✓, ✓), according to the usefulness of any given quote for my argument. Often, I'll scribble the letter "Q" in the margin beside such a quote (QQQ, QQ, Q) in the same fashion. If the author cites a work I want to include as part of my research, I'll simply write "rdg" in the margin. If he/she provides a key definition of a critical term, I'll write "def." If there's a quote I want to use in my introduction or conclusion, I'll write "Intro" or "concl."

This data-retrieval phase will be made that much easier if (when writing in the margins while you read) you establish some "labeling" system for your "graftings." These margin labels help direct each "grafting" to its proper place in the paper. Over the years, I've developed a trusty taxonomy with such simple labels as "lim" for a limitation to the argument I'm reading, or a +/- for a strength or weakness, or a "?" for a rhetorical question I want to raise, or various "sub-head" labels that become the "criteria" for developing my own thesis, and that help me direct marginal "graftings" to their proper place in the paper. These marginal labels become critical when the time arrives, as it inevitably must, to start "doing something" about this marginalia. Then begins the laborious process of transferring each one from the margins to the empty free-writing page—the second phase of this invention strategy.

If I read something that resonates with another text, I'll note the association in the margin. The following passage is from Donald Pizer's brilliant critical work on the expatriate writers of Paris:

Example 1

> "We can walk anywhere," Hemingway remarks. It is thus no wonder that he walks constantly in *A Moveable Feast* and that the trope of freedom through physical movement also dominates the powerfully affirmative portrayals of Paris as a city of growth for the artist in Anais Nin's diaries and Miller's *Tropic of Cancer* (11).

In the margin beside this passage, I wrote "ala Dublin walks of Stephen Dedalus in *Portrait*" (Joyce), because in my paper I want to develop the relationship between "walking" (or "nomadic consciousness") in the works of Joyce, Hemingway, Miller, and Nin. A second example helps to illustrate the process:

Example 2

> The Paris that Hemingway creates before his fall is thus a kind of writer's Eden in which the city's capacity to nourish his creative potency is richly productive. But his moment of luck is susceptible to time and thus change, with the idle rich and the seductive woman the agents of a fall from innocence.... He has become less the American innocent he was and more the bohemian expatriate he resisted becoming. And this, to his mind is a *fall from grace*. (19, my emphasis)

In the margins of this passage, I wrote the following:

movement from nourishment to corruption. A fall from his ideal self = profaned by hedonism and adultery. Results in weakened artistic impulse. Art sac. to life vs. opp."

These graftings were subsequently transferred to an empty page in my reader-response journal, where they were expanded upon in a journal free-write, as follows:

Example 3

> In *A Moveable Feast*, Hemingway is caught between the dual hungers for life and art. The first half narrates the primacy of art over life, in which Paris nourishes the creative impulse, in the same manner the "moveable feasts" he describes nourish his physical strength. When the equation shifts, however, it is art that is sacrificed to life (racing, gambling, debauchery, and adultery) with the resultant weakening of the creative impulse. Further, this conflict between art and life is one of the most fundamental conflicts in the careers of many artists, of which Hemingway's early career is an apt case study.

Example 4

On the following page is a passage from a primary text (Plato's *Phaedrus*), followed by William Covino's "reading" of it (*The Art of Wondering: A Revisionist Return to the History of Rhetoric 15*) commenting on this passage, surrounded in the margins by my own "graftings." Beginning with the left margin and reading counter-clockwise, those graftings read as follows (L= left, B= bottom, R= right, T=top):

L1: Socrates = mouthing Phaedrus. Orality as a vehicle for consuming Phaedrus. Satiric pastiche.

L2: Performative rhetoric vs. literal. Socrates is performing *Phaedrus*.

B: Phaedrus = trope for the modern student = pseudo knowledge, philosophy, language.

R: ? What is the relation 'tween love and rhetoric, desire and dialogue, sex and rhetoric?

T: Socrates' goal is to possess Phaedrus, consume him.

Having finished this critical reading and writing-in-the-margins phase, the laborious "retrieval" process then commences, going back over all the marginalia and transposing it to the blank, free-writing page, complete with page number and a word-perfect transcription of the quote to which the marginalia was "talking back." This done, the final (and often most pleasurable) phase can begin: pleasurable, because it is rooted in pure "discovery."

In essence, the reading and writing process are not sequential, but concomitant. Writing does not begin after reading, but during reading. Thus, by the time you finish your research reading, your paper has already begun. The process of talking back to texts in your own words and in their margins gives you, the writer, some much needed momentum, when the reading phase ends and the writing process commences in earnest. All that remains is to begin the process of transferring these marginal graftings, labels, and the quotes to which they refer to an empty page for further development, the essence of effective academic writing.

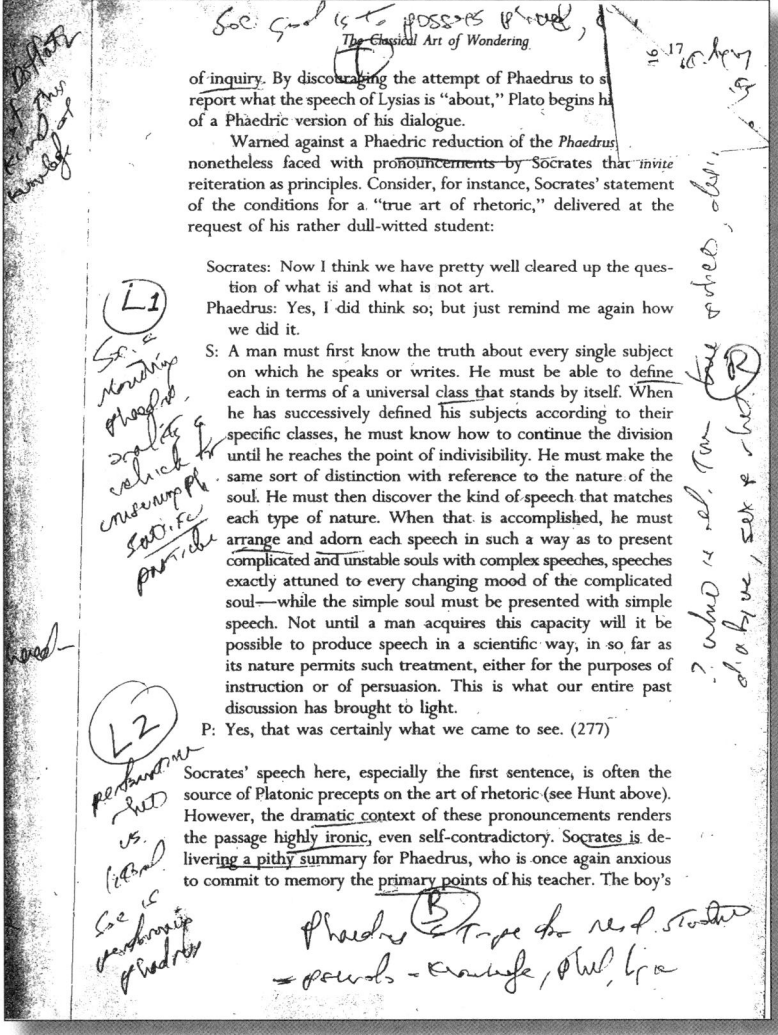

Free-Writing and Graftings

The transference of these graftings onto the empty page provides the opportunity for multiple free-writes, to start "jamming in ink," improvising off these graftings, letting them expand at will into further areas of development. These amplified graftings take me where I want to go (and need to go)—if my final draft is to have the fullness, depth, and concreteness effective academic writing demands. Free of the constraints of the margins, these "graftings" can now be developed at greater length—and development of your thesis is your number one priority beyond the paper's introduction.

Writing-to-Learn: Transferring Your Grafting

- Prioritize marginal graftings, with some kind of labeling system that ranks them.
- Transfer the quote (with page reference) to which the grafting was responding to an empty page in your reader-response journal.
- Transfer the first, most significant grafting to the same empty page, below the quote.
- Free-write on the "grafting," developing its ideas at greater length.
- Re-read your free-write, picking up any "leads" missed in the haste of the first pass.
- Return to margins, transferring the next most significant grafting to empty page of reader-response journal.
- Follow same process, free-writing to develop its ideas at greater length, re-reading to pick-up any "missed leads," then returning to margins for next most significant graft.
- In this manner, work your way through your most significant marginal writings.
- The result should be a mass of concrete development, albeit in rough-hewn form. In the next phase of the process (chapter four) you will begin turning these rough-hewn, extended free-writes into body paragraphs, first by grouping (cutting and pasting) the graftings according to their common themes, associations, or relation to your various criteria of development (sub-heads).
- This "cut and paste" process should result in multiple grafting

chains, or extended free-writes that are linked together, producing long "movements" of theme-related development, not unlike the process by which a musical composer develops the "movements" (sub-heads) of a symphony. From this rough-hewn mass of extended free-writes, your body paragraphs begin to take shape, resulting in a chain (or sequence) of related body paragraphs that "move in a common rhythm," (Piercy, "To Be of Use") as it were, developing a particular criterion of analysis (sub-head of thesis).

The point of all this free-writing is to put yourself into the "moment" of argumentative writing as soon and as continuously as possible. The process is messy and labor-intensive, but richly rewarding, insofar as it results in the thing every effective academic paper requires: density and depth of development. You have to be willing to surrender control over your writing in order to discover anything worthy of being controlled. As Elbow succinctly observes, "I finally learned I could write decent stuff if I let go of planning, control, and vigilance... I had to invite chaos" (xviii).

Obviously, this phase of the process should result in the exponential growth of your words on the page. Often it may seem as if you have invented a Frankenstein that controls you: a monster that must inevitably be wrestled into submission, cut down to size, harnessed and made to serve your ends. Even in the midst of hacking it down to a manageable size, it will continue to grow, to proliferate in places. The development and pruning phases are not absolutely distinct, or mutually exclusive. Often in your rewrites, both are occurring simultaneously: discovering side-by-side with deleting.

When this period of dramatic expansion exhausts itself or is arbitrarily ended by you, the labor of reasserting control over it begins in earnest. At this point, the writer borrows a page from Aristotle's rhetorical play-book: classification and division. "Like" goes with "like." In other words, you have left the Invention and Discovery phase in the rear view mirror and entered the Cut 'n Paste/Arrangement phase of the journey. Invention gives way to organization—though never absolutely. It is a matter of emphasis, as a shift occurs from discovery to arrangement. However, even in the midst of this "cut and paste," reorganization phases, you should always remain attuned to the "Eureka!" moment, when you discover a means of strengthening your argument: whether through an apt analogy (metaphor), a new line of reasoning, a refutation of a counter argument, a personal anecdote that enlivens your thesis, a better place for a particular quote, or a further means of explicating a quote, etc. I will leave further discussion of Arrangement/Development to a later chapter, keeping the primary focus of this chapter on the Invention/Discovery phase of the process.

Writing-to-Learn: Free-Writing on Graftings

- At home, in journal, free-write in the margins of whatever course reading has been assigned (or in the margins of your own research sources). Photocopy library materials (articles, book chapters, etc.) so you can free-write in the margins at your will. Agree or disagree with a point being made, a line of reasoning; write a question in response to it; question its claims and assumptions; ask "yeah, but what about. . . ?"; identify a quote you want to use in your paper and implement a system for ranking these quotes (*, **, ***); note an effective use of metaphor, etc.
- Photocopy a page of text with your marginal comments and share in group, decoding any short hand or symbols for your peers.
- At home, continue to free-write in margins.
- Go back over your marginal responses, identifying the strongest ones with some system of ranking.
- Transpose one of these marginal responses to an empty page in your reader-response journal. Above it, record the quote to which it was responding with a page reference.
- Free write on the marginal response, developing its meanings at greater length.
- Re-read your free-write, picking up any "missed leads."
- Share in group, decoding its short hand and symbols.
- Volunteers share aloud with class.

- At home, in journal, continue working your way through your marginal responses, transposing the strongest ones to an empty page in reader-response journal, in tandem with the quote to which it refers, with page reference.
- Free-write on each of these marginal responses, developing their meanings at length.
- "Cut and paste" these extended free-writes, organizing them into thematically-related groups.
- Rank the paragraphs in these groups in the best chronological order, using a numbering system.
- Beginning with #1, rewrite these free-writes from beginning to end, starting a new paragraph each time you come to a new #. Look for opportunities to tighten your prose and further develop any associations between them. In this way, you begin to develop each criterion of analysis (subhead) with an extended sequence of paragraphs, grouped by virtue of their "relatedness," or thematic association with the particular criterion of analysis.

V. The Reader-Response Journal

In addition to writing in the margins of a text, another effective invention technique is to keep a "reader-response" journal, in which you first transcribe a key quote and then respond to it—perhaps strongly agreeing or disagreeing with it, using the "yeah, but what about. . ." as a prompt, explicating its meanings, unpacking a metaphor, or otherwise responding as you did in the margins, but at greater length. By all means, if you strike a strong vein of response, don't arbitrarily stop. Rather, write for as long as you're inspired or able to. Often, your best ideas/insights will occur in these "heat of the moment" responses. A few of them cobbled together form "islands" of meaning, which when linked may become part of the body of your paper. Always think "two birds with one stone" when reading and when keeping a reader-response journal: "I'm not only fulfilling the assignment of making a journal entry, but have already begun the process of writing my paper." As with the marginalia, these journal responses become even larger graftings, once transposed to the empty page—where they become suitable raw material for further working and development—in short, for body paragraphs.

This is also an effective strategy for initiating a "dialogue" with a text as a pretext for developing your own text. In other words, you discover your voice through an Other's, or through dialogue with an Other's. Knowledge (meaning) is the result of an exchange, a negotiation between Other and Self, (pre)text and text.

Writing in the margins of a text and keeping a reader-response journal are effective ways to begin and to develop a paper, for the simple reason that they put you into the moment of writing, immediately and continuously—as opposed to traditional, think-before-you-write strategies, such as outlining, which defer that moment. The journal, like the margins of a text, is a safe place to play with words and ideas: a place that privileges practice and experimentation—for grade-wise, the stakes are low. There's nothing to lose—but your mind, which sometimes must be lost in order to be found. As strategies of invention and discovery, the reader-response journal and writing-in-the-margins possess another key advantage: an early start-up for your paper. Instead of deferring writing until after everything has been read, these activities front-load the writing moment, which occurs while one is reading. In other words, while your peers are waiting until the reading is finished and the writing assignment given to begin their papers, you have been writing all along, from the moment the first reading is assigned. When it comes time to "start" writing the paper, instead of having to start from scratch, you will already have a data-base with which to begin—because you've already done the "leg-work" of data-collection. Consequently, when the readings are done, you are able to "hit the ground running," as it were, because you already have pages of substantive responses to texts, with quotes and page references—in short, you already have the first draft of your paper.

You are ahead of the game: always a nice place to be in the academic stampede to multiple deadlines. Develop your "readings" of the texts you read while you are reading them—not after. Write to "read."

Reader-Response Journal: Student Sample

Quote: "The ferocity with which some faculty insist that today's students are vastly inferior to those of their own generation makes one wonder whether social change alone can account for such dramatic decline" (Parker Palmer, 40-41).

Response: (reading against-the-grain of the quote): "While it's undoubtedly true that teachers bear some responsibility for what happens (or fails to happen) in the classroom, it's incredibly disingenuous to suggest that students play no part in the situation. The education equation has two main variables: the instructor and the student. Both have responsibilities and if both meet their responsibilities then the equation works. If there's an imbalance on either end, however, the equation breaks down. Palmer overlooks an important factor here, and that is the role that education, particularly higher education, has come to play in our society. Today, everyone is expected to go to college... the result has been a massive influx of students who are unprepared...."

Implications: These reader-responses afford students the opportunity to model their own critical voices in response to another text, to try out arguments—which may work their way into an essay. Unconstrained by the margins of a text, they allow for greater play of mind than do marginal "graftings." In tandem with these graftings, however, they generate the critical "back talk," and help develop the strong interpretative voice that is the essence of effective academic writing.

Conclusion: Theorizing "Write First" Invention Strategies

> "Conceiving of writing as the act of recording what one thinks, may well be the most frustrating possible approach to writing because it presumes that some way of 'thinking' outside and prior to writing exists."
>
> —NEEL, 130

The process of "talking back" to a text in its margins as a springboard into a series of free-writes, I've found to be a useful strategy for inventing or discovering my arguments. It guarantees that my writing occurs in the context of a "conversation" with another text, giving it an inter-textual relevance. Effective academic writing does not occur in an intellectual isolation chamber, but in the "conversational" space between the texts of Self and Other. So, "talk back" to the texts you read, early and often. Then, instead of having to pull a paper out of thin air, instead of starting with nothing, you will already possess a rhetorical quarry from which to rough hew your paper. As Jasper Neel observes, "no matter how much a text struggles to keep itself pure and different from other texts, it originates as a weaving of prior texts. It must graft itself onto something else in order to become itself." Neel's concept of the "graft" speaks to the very nature of writing: "that process of inserting something alien into a pre-existing host" (128). Neel continues:

> Referring to his own writing as a sort of inserted, grafted reading, Derrida says, "It is necessary to read and re-read those in whose wake I write, the 'books' in whose margins and between whose lines I mark out and read a text. . . ." Derrida's texts operate in the rupture created when he inserts his text into another text. . . . "Therefore, extraction, graft, extension," Derrida explains, "this is what I call, according to the process I have just described, writing" (qtd. in Neel, 128).

Writing occurs in the space between Self and Other; meaning emerges from the interplay of your words with another's. Writing does not occur in a social vacuum, is not, as Karen Burke Lefevre asserts, a "private activity carried out through introspection" (*Invention as a Social Act* 12). Rather, it occurs, as Lev Vygotsky observes, in a "zone of proximal development" with the other, in which "intellectual growth is contingent on. . . mastering the social means of thought" (94). The writerly "I," as Martin Buber avers, is an "I of infinite conversation" (qtd. in Lefevre 10). This social view of invention extends back to the ancient Greeks, insofar as the "I of Plato always invents in awareness of the 'Thou'" (Buber, qtd. in Lefevre 12).

A second fundamental assumption informing this theory of invention pertains to the critical relation between thought and language. Traditionally, writing teachers assumed that thought preceded language, and therefore it was essential to think before you wrote. Peter Elbow summarizes this approach as follows: "First you figure out your meaning, then you put it into language. . . . First try and figure out what you want to say; don't start writing till you do; make a plan; use an outline; begin writing only afterward" (14). This attitude was based on the assumption that writing was an expression of thought. Classroom methods that reflected this assumption (such as outlining) were consequently privileged. Entire theoretical schools emerged privileging this view (Piaget), exerting a profound influence on education from early childhood programs through college. In the 1960s and 70s, theorists and compositionists from Vygotsky (*Thought and Language*, 1962) to Elbow (*Writing Without Teachers*, 1973) began challenging this assumption, bringing it under radical attack, advocating that the relationship between thought and language was the exact opposite: that language shapes thought. As Elbow asserts, "this idea of writing is backwards. . . . Meaning is not what you start out with, but what you end up with" (15).

Without adequate time for the invention and discovery phase of the writing process, a thesis-driven, research paper does, indeed, devolve into a mere "academic" exercise—in which form trumps content and thought follows formulaic patterns. The play of mind follows the play of language. Writing in the margins of an Other's text and keeping a reader-response journal give language the "play" it needs in order to form thought.

Climactic Assessment

Two of the greatest problems that plague student writers are the intellectual inertia that must be surmounted to commence an academic paper and the dense variety of content needed to develop it. The strategies modeled in this chapter, developed from experience, field-tested in diverse classroom settings, are designed to overcome these problems, as follows:

- Collaborative invention strategies
- Webbing
- Free-writing
- Writing in the margins
- Reader-Response Journal

With these rhetorical strategies in his or her "tool kit," the academic writer is better positioned to meet with success, not only in his or her first-year writing courses, but throughout his or her academic career—in any course that privileges thesis-driven, evidence-based, argumentative writing. Possessing strategies that put you immediately, continuously, and productively into the moment of academic writing is essential for success. However, before you can respond to the texts that serve as (pre)texts for your own words, you must first find them—and to do that you must know where and how to search for them. The course readings required and provided by the instructor are merely the starting point of the argumentative journey. To continue and complete it, you must possess or develop effective search (research) strategies of your own. The next chapter models effective strategies for "researching a researchable thesis," which are as vital to your rhetorical "tool kit" (and therefore to your success as an academic writer) as the strategies of invention and discovery.

CHAPTER TWO

"And I Quote": Researching a Researchable Thesis

> "What we need in the knowledge industries are people who know how to absorb and analyze and integrate . . . and effectively convey information—and who know how to use information to bring real value to everything they undertake."
> —ANTHONY COMPER, PRESIDENT, BANK OF MONTREAL (TO GRADUATING CLASS, UNIVERSITY OF TORONTO, 1999)

Information Literacy: The Search for Relevant Intelligence

Whereas invention and discovery strategies (free-writing, reader-response, collaborative feedback groups) bring the writer's own voice decisively into play, research is intended to bring the informed (and therefore persuasive) voices of others into the writing "moment," in support of the writer's voice. In persuasive discourse, this is a critical, if not essential, rhetorical strategy. The aforementioned quote is significant insofar as it concisely sets forth the goals of information literacy (research). What, precisely, is meant by "information literacy"? As defined by the American Library Association (ALA), information literacy is a "set of abilities requiring individuals to 'recognize when information is needed and have the ability to locate, evaluate, and use effectively the needed information" (American Library Association, qtd. in *Information Literacy. . . Higher Education* 2). This chapter will model strategies for effectively and efficiently realizing these goals. As the ALA asserts, Information literacy also is increasingly important in the contemporary environment of rapid technological change and proliferating information resources . . . [in which] individuals are faced with diverse, abundant information choices—in their academic studies, in the workplace, and in their personal lives. . . . [I]ncreasingly, information comes to individuals in unfiltered formats, raising questions about its authenticity, validity, and reliability. . . [that] poses new challenges for individuals evaluating and understanding it. . . . The sheer abundance of information will not in itself create a more informed citizenry without a complementary cluster of abilities necessary to use the information effectively (2).

To efficiently locate and effectively utilize information in this environment, the student researcher needs to possess a "cluster of abilities," as follows:

- Identify and access the needed information.
- Evaluate/ assess the information and its sources critically.
- Extract the information.
- Incorporate selected information into your own text.
- Document the sources of information.
- Disseminate the information to your peers.

These are the abilities that will be emphasized in this chapter. This research process, moreover, reinforces the writing process insofar as it favors and develops critical thinking skills, by prompting the researcher to assess at every stage of the journey the value, relevance, and validity of the information accessed during the search. Each piece of information is weighed, as it were, on a set of (mental) scales that assess its usefulness in light of several criteria: has the information been "reviewed" before publication; is the source legitimate; and is it relevant to your writing focus? Hence, the information is "filtered" through this process of "critical discernment and reasoning"(3), which alone warrants its citation in a document. Credibility as a writer is not something to be compromised, inasmuch as it enables the writer to accomplish his or her foremost goal: persuasion of the reader. Yet, nothing compromises credibility swifter than flawed sources. If the old adage is true that you may "judge a man by the company he keeps," then it is equally true that you may judge a writer's credibility by the sources he/she cites.

More specifically, this research process strengthens and utilizes a "cluster of abilities," as follows:

- Development of a research plan or strategy.
- Identification/definition of key terms.
- Development of information-retrieval strategies, including use of internal organizers such as table of contents, indexes, user's guides, etc.
- Development of a system for organizing information.
- Development of information-extraction skills (photocopy, electronic copy/paste protocols, direct transcription/note taking).
- Identification of critical gaps in the research base (working bibliography) of a given writing project.
- Development of summary and paraphrase abilities.
- Development of discipline-specific citation skills (MLA, APA, Chicago).
- Development of a working bibliography throughout the research process.
- Development of critical assessment abilities regarding the validity, reliability, and relevancy of sources, as well as the strengths and weaknesses of a source's argument.
- Development of ability to recognize "the cultural, [historical]... or other context within which the information was created, and understands the impact of context on interpreting the information" (11).
- Development of the ability to think associatively, to recognize relevant associations between sources.
- Development of a source's significance or relevance to the particular writing focus during the research moment (writing in the

margins, or free-writing in journal responses to the sources).
- Development of a ranking/labeling system regarding the relative usefulness of sources.

Writing-to-Learn: Research

The Research Portfolio

During the research process you will keep a research portfolio, which will include the following:
- The *central research question(s)*
- A brief description of the origin/genesis of your focus, of your interest in it
- Selective entries from your *research journal/log*
- A *research plan*
- A working *bibliography* (works cited)
- A brief description of your *information retrieval and extraction* methods
- A brief description of your *system for organizing* the information retrieved and extracted
- A brief, but substantive *review of the most relevant criticism*
- Reader-response free-writes to selected quotes, in which you develop the significance/relevance of the quote to your thesis;
- A *paraphrase* and a *summary* of a selected quote
- An entry in which you *integrate a quote* into your own words in four different ways
- An entry in which your *integrate a block quote* into your own text
- A brief description of the system you used to *assess the worthiness* or credibility of your sources

Follow-Up
- At the end of your project, you will give a presentation, draw-

ing on the various documents in your research portfolio. The portfolio will be turned in for a grade along with your research paper.

The Research Journal/Log

In your *research journal/log* you will make two kinds of entries:

- A weekly record of the "research activities related to information seeking."
- Reflective entries on the research experience that describe frustrations and failures, epiphanies and successes, and that narrate the evolution of the information search, that record any interesting anecdotes in the process, etc. As always, number and date each entry.
- In group, share a *reflective entry* from your journal, in which you describe a success, an epiphany (or Eureka!) moment, your frustrations, (a research librarian who was indifferent or inaccessible, a book that wasn't where it was supposed to be on the shelf though "not checked out," running out of change at the photocopy machine, etc.).
- Share an entry in which you describe the research activities undertaken.

Getting Started: The Central Research Question(s)

The first task of academic writing is deciding on a focus (crafting a working, researchable thesis) then framing that focus as a central question. The researcher's inquiry will be driven by this question (or set of questions). Hence, research is conducted in the spirit of an *Inquiry*. In this, the researcher possesses a natural advantage, for the mind is naturally inquisitive: it wants to delve beneath the surface of things, to find out "what makes something (or someone) tick." This in-born inquisitiveness is a useful and steadfast ally throughout the research process. Thus, it helps to approach the search for "relevant intelligence" in the spirit of a sleuth, a detective, or an academic "private eye." The book shelves, periodical racks, and electronic databases are the sites where the "field work" is conducted in the search for useable evidence. The search, however, commences with the "framing of a significant question or set of questions," which it then seeks to answer (*Reinventing Undergraduate Education*, qtd. in ALA 4).

A Writing to-Learn Sequence: The Central Research Question and Criteria of Development

- In journal, record your central research question(s).
- Share in group.
- Rewrite, incorporating any useful feedback.
- In group, generate a list of criteria by which to develop the central research focus for every member of the group.
- As a group, radically limit the number of these criteria, to the 3 or 4 most relevant, significant, or researchable criteria.
- Rank these final criteria in reverse order, weakest to strongest,
- "Recorder" keeps a master list for each member's research focus.
- "Reporter" shares with class.

These criteria are what narrow and define the scope of your research. All research should be directed to locating, assessing, extracting, and integrating information that relates to these criteria.

Having framed the focus of the inquiry, the next move is to put yourself-as-writer "into the moment" of writing, by plunging directly into the invention and discovery phases (employing a combination of strategies in Chapter One). Subsequent to (or in tandem with) this invention/discovery "moment" is the research phase of the process. In conjunction with the invention/discovery/revision process, the research phase is the primary means by which a researchable thesis is developed. If the invention/discovery phase brings your own "voice" decisively into the discussion, then the research phase brings other (expert) voices into the argument in support of your own.

Where to find these other critical voices? Once found, how to integrate them into your paper, how to blend their words with your own? Having found and integrated their words into your paper, how do you give them proper attribution? And most importantly, how do you develop their relevance to your thesis? Finally, having done all this, how do you format the "Works Cited" page that lists your sources? These are the writing issues this chapter will address.

The Research Plan

- In journal, write a draft of your research plan that includes strategies for finding library and internet sources. Be as inclusive as you can. How will you go about finding the necessary information?
- Share in group.
- Modify your plan, incorporating any useful ideas from your group.
- Visit the research librarian, modifying your plan to include any useful suggestions, leads, etc.
- Develop a working list of relevant web sites to visit.
- Seek out and interview an expert in the field, for relevant sources, or ways to find these relevant sources (schedule an interview with a professor or graduate student).
- Share your refined "research plan" with group.
- Include in your research portfolio.

Putting Your Research Plan Into Action

Beginning in the library, start systematically locating sources, following the "leads" in your plan. This plan should include "leads" for finding books, chapters in books, and articles related to your research focus. Be as exhaustive as necessary to meet the scope of your research project. In conducting research on a thesis, the trick is to develop methods that are as time-efficient as they are thorough. The goal is to get in and get out, with a minimum of wasted time: to locate the sources you need without wasting hours searching for them. This chapter models research methods as effective as they are efficient. Few of us want (or can afford) to spend endless hours fruitlessly searching the shelves and databases for sources. Consequently, before you commence researching your thesis, you must develop an effective *search strategy* for finding the relevant sources—a process that I refer to as "The Search for Relevant Intelligence in the Universe of the Thesis." And at times, the realm of Research can, indeed, seem as limitless and strange as a parallel universe to our own: one in which the novice researcher can easily become lost, through which he/she can wander in an aimless quest for Relevant Intelligence, following dead ends, wasting valuable hours in an unproductive search for sources, sans the proper search beacons to guide the writer to those particular sources that inform any given thesis. We've all encountered those "lost souls" wandering aimlessly amidst the shelves (or scrolling endlessly through the "virtual shelves" of the electronic library), cross-eyed from a search for relevant intelligence as frustrating as it is fruitless—trying to shake fruit from a barren tree-of-knowledge.

This Relevant Intelligence is out there; you just have to know where to find it.

To write a thesis-driven paper and NOT include the most definitive source(s) on the subject, those that have most influenced other writers, or a recent source that is proving influential or that brings a fresh perspective to an old debate, is an egregious error of omission that undercuts your credibility as an academic writer—compromising the primary effect of your writing: the ability to persuade a reader. But where to find these "must have" sources, these critical voices in the debate—and more importantly, how to find them?

Entering the (Critical) Conversation: The Working Bibliography

Writing an effective academic paper on a researchable subject is, to a large degree, a matter of entering a critical "conversation"—one, which (if it is of any significance to the subject) is usually an ongoing discussion. There are several strategies for finding the major "voices" in any on-going debate on a given subject.

Old School Methods: Browse the Shelves

One of my first moves is to simply locate the shelves in the library that house the books related to my subject, and "go shopping." Using a key-word (subject/author/title) search, I first browse the library "holdings" on the subject electronically, jotting down the call numbers to those that look promising. Once amidst the shelves, I locate these. Then I quickly search the *table of contents* for "relevant intelligence" (stuff I can possibly use). After this, I flip directly to the *works cited*, and scan the sources this writer used, noting in my research journal the ones that seem promising. Always keep the electronic-print out of these sources because each entry possesses the definitive bibliographic information you need for your works cited page, and nothing can be more frustrating than having to return to the library an hour before your paper is due in search of the city or year, the volume number or inclusive pages of a source you have quoted.

What I am most vigilant for at this point are the sources (authors) whose names keep appearing in works cited lists. This is a telltale clue to this source's centrality to the scholarly conversation. I search for the sources everyone else seems to be citing. Chances are, if a given source appears on several works cited lists, it is a "must read," which I add to my own working bibliography. Then I go find this source, check its works cited page, and check the sources that informed its inquiry. These works cited pages are like beacons that guide you directly to the "conversations" that have been (or are being) waged on a given subject. An effective, time-efficient means of determining the *critical cruxes* being debated on any subject: the hot-button issues, at any given "moment" of a critical debate.

During this phase of the search, the researcher begins to get a sense of the "conversation(s)" occurring in the subject area, or a sense of how that "conversation" has evolved over the decades, if not centuries: its various permutations and paradigm shifts. You begin to "home in" on those sources that make for a good match with your own particular focus. With any luck, you head to the check-out desk (or photocopy machine) with an arm load of books. Instead of checking out a source, often it is more convenient to photocopy just the chapter you want to read (*and mark up*) as part of the essential "talking back" phase of the development process. If photocopying, be sure to copy the title and copyright pages.

Useful Sources/Books

Guide to Reference Books (10th ed): A guide to all reference works in existence in all fields up to 1984. Includes bibliographies, indexes, guides, encyclopedias, atlases, serial publications, government publications, handbooks, histories, etc. Extensive author-subject-title index. Arranged by subject headings. Start search with table of contents and index. Contains brief, insightful evaluations that are useful for developing research leads.

Books in Print: The definitive bibliography source. A trade bibliography of books published in the U.S. Accesses 30k U.S. publishers. Has 13k new titles. Alphabetized by author/title. Best starting point is the Subject Guide, which provides quick access to all titles. Useful for developing a working bibliography. Note: see the *CB Index*: Counterpart to B.I.P. for non-American authors.

WWW.Amazon.com: for most recent books (10 years) in a given field. Accessed under "search" with key words (i.e., "Travel Writing"). Useful for developing up-to-date working bibliography on a given subject.

Index to Book Reviews in the Humanities: Index of first resort for current reviews (within 6-8 months) of publication. Indexes 600 periodicals in the humanities and several thousand book titles. Alphabetical by author of the book reviewed. A complement to *Book Review Digest*.

Book Review Digest: A useful, one-stop shopping guide for conducting quick searches of relevant books. Contains excerpts to current English language reviews of selected current works of fiction/non-fiction, appearing in 90 periodicals. Reviews are arranged alphabetically by author of book reviewed. Indicates how books were received when published.

Contemporary Authors: A biographic and bibliographic guide to current authors and works (new and/or obscure) that includes living writers in many fields from all countries (96k writers). Covers fiction, non-fiction, poetry, journalism, drama, cinema, television, and miscellaneous fields. Alphabetically by author. *CA* and *CLC* are inter-indexed. Best starting point is latest Cumulative Index to locate volume and page # for a given author.

Library of Congress Subject Index: An international subject index to books, which is a list and a guide. Provides list of subject headings indexed. Arranged alphabetically by subject heading. Useful for generating ideas/leads in a subject search, for refining focus of inquiry, developing sub-categories of inquiry, etc.

MLA International Bibliography: An international bibliography of books and articles by scholars and critics of all nations on the literature of all nations. Available on-line. Best starting point is in the Annotated Classified Listing (a separate volume containing other 5 volumes). Use Subject Index for cross references (separate volume).

The Search Continues: Journal Articles

Having located the relevant books in the library, where does the Search for Relevant Intelligence lead next? Journal articles are often the richest source of "relevant intelligence" for any thesis-driven paper. No working bibliography is complete without a diligent search of the journal articles relevant to your thesis. These can be accessed easily and electronically via a simple journal subject/title search. Again, you will be led to the most relevant articles by the works cited lists of the library book holdings. More will turn up from your electronic search. To make your working bibliography complete, you will need to find the most influential books and articles on your subject in the last ten years. Relevant books can be found by a simple search on Amazon.com. Many of these articles you will find in the library's journal racks, or in the shelves that hold the back issues or hard-bound volumes. A treasure trove of relevant intelligence lies there waiting to be found. Books not included in your library's holdings can be obtained through interlibrary loan. Again, with the relevant journals in hand, head for the photocopy machine and begin copying. Now your working bibliography is starting to take shape. You are only part way home, however.

Useful Sources

1. *Academic Search Premier* (Library home page).
2. *Ulrich's International Periodical Directory: A Classified Guide to Current Periodicals* (Foreign and Domestic), with a subject-title index. The most comprehensive listing of periodicals in almost all subject areas (118k entries), with a list of journal abbreviations. On-line since 1981.
3. *Poole's Index to Periodical Literature:* A subject index only. 2.5k articles in 470 periodicals of the 19th century. (US & Britain).
4. *MLA Directory of Periodicals.*
5. *Arts & Humanities Citation Index*: A multi-disciplinary index of citations to journals in the Arts and Humanities. Indexes 6100 journals. Current articles can be accessed through the older works they cite. On-line since 1983. Useful for recent writers, tracing debates on controversial issues, and for working up a full bibliography.
6. *Union List of Serials:* A location guide to holdings of 900 libraries. Includes any periodical ever published. Includes 150k different serials before 1949. Not useful for subject searches; must know title. Indispensable for any search involving periodicals, particularly in American Literature. Arranged alphabetically by title. Useful for generating leads to individual volume and

page #s of a given article. Facilitates search for periodicals to which you don't have direct access.

New School Searches

Internet Intelligence (From "Use Computer Technology to Enhance Research and Writing" in Searches (9-12).

Today's Web-browsing and word-processing programs offer a number of features that can make your research collection, organization, and revising much easier than recording information by handwriting, as follows.

Create Links to Your Sources with Bookmarks (Favorites)

Internet Explorer and other Web-browsing programs have a built-in feature to create bookmarks for pages you would like to return to in the future, and you can use this feature to create a folder of links for a particular research project. In Internet Explorer, bookmarks are called *Favorites*. Add a source to your list of *Favorites* by following these steps:

1. Direct your browser to the page that you want to add to your list.
2. Using the *Favorites* menu, click *Add to Favorites*.
3. When prompted, name the source.
4. Continue this process with other Web sources.
5. To open the link to a favorite source, use the *Favorites* menu, and click the page you want to open.
6. You can organize your list of sources by moving the links into subfolders. Using the *Favorites* menu, click on *Organize Favorites*.
7. When prompted, click *Create Folder*, type a name for the folder (perhaps the research topic), and then press ENTER.
8. Drag the links for sources in the list to the appropriate folders. Instead of dragging, you can also use the *Move to Folder* button.

"Cut and Paste" Text to Facilitate Note Taking

Like many other writers, you can use "cut and paste" computer technology to make note taking easy. For example, say you want to copy a section of a *Salon* article about recycling from the magazine's Web site:

1. Open a new document in Microsoft Word.
2. Display the text of your source in Internet Explorer.
3. Highlight a section of the text you want to save and use the *Edit* menu in Microsoft Word to copy the text.
4. Paste the text into your Microsoft Word screen and put quote marks around the quoted text. Add bibliographic information about the source to the top of the Word file and your own remarks about the quote.

You can continue to cut and paste sections of the article into the document and intersperse them with your own comments. You may want to put quoted material in italics to distinguish it clearly from your own words. Later, you can convert quotes into summaries or paraphrases, if you wish.

Use Microsoft Word's Comment Feature to Label Quotes

One problem students often experience, when working with material from sources, is that source material is pasted as quotes into a draft, and information about the source can become lost or confused. If you use Microsoft's *Comment* feature to label each section associated with a particular source, that information is transferred when the wording is pasted into a new document. For example, if you were working on your notes about the *Salon* article, you can easily add bibliographic information about the source of the quote.

1. Highlight the portion of the text to be associated with the comment.
2. Go to the *Insert* menu and select *Comment*. In the box that appears below, type or cut and paste bibliographical information

to be associated with that particular text. When you move the highlighted text to another document or a different location in a document, the comment will still be present and give bibliographical information. You can also use the *Comment* feature to ask yourself questions or leave suggestions for future revision. Windows XP utilizes the *View* menu and *Markup* feature to display *Comments*.

Use Email to Transmit Paper Drafts

Have you ever lost a draft of a paper or other assignment because the disk you used to save your document became corrupted, and your document would not open? Of course, you can have two disks and record each draft of your paper on both disks which would reduce the risk of losing a paper draft. Another popular way to prevent the loss of your work is to email each draft to yourself as an email attachment. This second method has two advantages: If you are working on your paper both at home and at a computer on campus, you can transport the paper back and forth by email, eliminating the disk problem. Also, if you do not erase the emails containing your drafts as attachments, you have a record of each draft in case you want to retrieve text from an earlier draft.

Most email programs, such as Yahoo! Mail, allow you to easily attach a text file as an attachment. Simply display the compose message screen, usually by clicking on *New Message* or *Compose Message*, **and** fill in the *To:* box with your own email address. Then click on *Attachments* and follow the program's instructions for attaching a file. Send the email, and it will appear in your email message inbox.

Locate Assignments and Join Discussions on Your Class Web Site

More and more professors are making use of Web-based technology to deliver all or part of a college course. On the simplest level, a professor may post a syllabus containing course policies and due dates on a Web page. At the most complex, a class is actually held in cyberspace, either in hybrid part-classroom/part-online format or completely online.

In many cases, the online course components may require a login and password to access materials. This policy restricts the use of the text, images, sound, and other types of files to the instructor and the students, thus protecting the professor's work and also allowing certain third-party copyrighted works to be included under the copyright "fair use" policy.

Your instructor may make use of course management software (CMS) such as WebCT or Blackboard to deliver the course content. The software allows instructors easily to post syllabi, assignments, and other files. In addition, CMS includes interactive features such as real-time chat rooms, email, and discussion boards that allow you to communicate with classmates and the instructor.

Integrating Sources Into Your Text
Paraphrase and Summary

A critical skill in the researcher's rhetorical tool bag is the ability to concisely and accurately summarize and paraphrase sources. These are useful strategies for several reasons: they make for economical use of space, adding density to your paper; they add emphasis by eliminating lack-luster quotes, while at the same time adding concrete development by accessing relevant intelligence in your own words (with proper attribution, of course); they add variety to your writing by integrating source material into your text in diverse ways; and finally, the summarizing skills that are honed to a fine edge will pay real dividends when it comes time to craft a review of criticism as concise as it is cogent.

Paraphrase

An honest paraphrase is one in which the ideas of a source are stated in the essay writer's *own words*. A paraphrase is usually based on a brief excerpt of one or two sentences and presents the same information as the original passage. Though approximating the original passage in length, it is written in your own words. A line-by-line conversion from the author's words into your own is a useful means to generate a paraphrase. As with the summary, to

Evaluating Information Found On the Web

There is much information available to researchers on the Web. It is available 24/7, and in some cases, easy to find. But before you use only information from the Web, you must evaluate it.

1. Evaluate the site.

Look first at the site on which the document is located. Who is the sponsor of the site? Are there lots of pictures? This could be a hint that the site is not scholarly in nature. The URL (or address) for a site offers quite a few clues. Check the domain for starters. A .com site will often feature ads. Does the document you obtained support those ads? A .org site often has a biased point of view. If the information you have located strongly supports that point of view, be cautious. Sites with .gov in the URL will often give reliable statistics, as will .us sites for state governments. Many .edu sites offer educational research but often also provide space for faculty and students to express their personal ideas. If you found your www.library.unlv.edu), you can be confident that your information is the same as the print equivalent.

2. Evaluate the document.

There are five common criteria for evaluating material found on the Web:

- **Authority.** Can you determine who wrote it? Is there an email address given so that you may contact the author? Can you determine the author's credentials and/or affiliation?
- **Authenticity.** Are the sources well documented? Is there a bibliography? Is there any evidence that the document is forged or altered?
- **Appropriateness.** Try to discover the intended audience for this document. Is it too technical or too elementary for your research?
- **Timeliness.** Can you determine the date the document was written or published? Is the information too dated?
- **Objectivity.** Why do you think the author published this information? To argue a position? To sway others to a particular point of view? To explain or to report events? To inform and give facts and data?

Because of the vast amount of information available on the Web, every document you select must be evaluated before you can use the information for your research with confidence. With a little practice, however, you'll find yourself able to apply the checklist and insure that you are using quality resources. Remember to accurately cite every Web resource you use.

avoid plagiarism, the author and passage must be given proper attribution, in the same manner as a direct quote.

Rhetorical Strategies: Substitution and Flipping-the-Script

The following, five-step process is a simple, useful technique for paraphrasing:

- Using the same sentence-structure as the author, substitute your own words for his or hers.
- Work your way through the passage, line-by-line.
- Collect your sentences into a draft.
- Rewrite this draft, using your own sentence-structure: reversing the order of subject and verbs; combining sentences; changing the order of the sentences.
- Check the relevant citation technique at the end of this chapter (MLA, APA, Chicago) and give the source its proper attribution.

Example: Original Source (from Alexis de Tocqueville, *Democracy in America*)

> "No political form has hitherto been discovered that is equally favorable to the prosperity and development of all the classes into which society is divided. These classes continue to form, as it were, so many distinct communities in the same nation; and experience has shown that it is not less dangerous to place the fate of these classes exclusively in the hands of any one of them. . . . When the rich alone govern, the interest of the poor is always endangered; and when the poor make laws, that of the rich incurs very serious risks. The advantage of democracy does not consist, therefore, as has sometimes been asserted, in favoring prosperity for all, but simply in contributing to the wellbeing of the greatest number" (248-249).

Student Paraphrase

> "De Tocqueville says that no form of government in history

has been uniformly beneficial to all classes of society. He maintains that both the rich and the poor, when in control of government, pass laws favorable to their class and repressive toward the other. Accordingly, the virtue of a democracy is that it benefits the majority, not that it benefits the whole" (*Democracy in America*, 248-249).

Summary

A summary condenses information from the original source. It presents key ideas and important information, omitting unnecessary details. It is written in your own words, and accurately represents the key ideas of the source being summarized. Though the information is put into your own words, the source must still be properly cited. Whether directly quoting, or indirectly summarizing and paraphrasing another text, the goal is to smoothly integrate it into your own text—to generate a seamless splice between another's words and your own. The list of verbs on the next page is a handy reference guide with which to facilitate this process. Note, that when quoting, summarizing, or paraphrasing other writers, they are cited in the *present tense*: asserts, avers, affirms, attests, etc. In other words, they are cited as if they are always and forever living in the *eternal present* by virtue of their words.

What to Include in a Summary

- The author's *thesis* (focus): what is he/she arguing or trying to prove.
- How he or she *develops* that thesis.
- The *limitations* of their argument.
- Its most original or significant elements, what it *contributes* to the overall conversation.

Rhetorical Strategies: Reduction and Extraction

This strategy involves reducing the passage in question to its central point and how it is developed, as follows:

- Underline the most important sentences or make notes on them;
- Write a sentence that states the main point (assertion, claim);
- Write a sentence for each of the main criteria by which this central claim (thesis) is developed;
- Bring your individual sentences together to form a draft;
- Revise and edit for clarity.

acknowledges	concludes	enumerates	offers
adds	confirms	establishes	points out
analyzes	considers	expresses	presents
argues	contends	finds	professes
asks	continues	illustrates	proposes
assents	declares	implies	protests
asserts	defines	informs	recalls
assures	denounces	insists	reiterates
attests	describes	introduces	relates
claims	details	lists	remarks
clarifies	disagrees	maintains	repeats
comments	discusses	mentions	reports
compares	emphasizes	notes	reveals
concedes	explains	observes	says
sees	speculates	suggests	thinks
shows	states	tells	writes

Summary: Student Sample 1 (Sociology of Aging)

"How to Survive the First Year," by Kelly Green, appeared in the *Wall Street Journal* (June 9, 2003). Based on dozens of responses from people around the country, Kelly reports that the first year of retirement is often difficult for unexpected reasons. Disorientation was a common feeling among many of the responses. Kelly suggests different ways to ease the adjustment process, from shifting personal attitudes and outlooks to modifying spending habits and the construction of social networks."

Follow-up: Instruct students to underline the most important words or sentence in this summary, then craft a *one-sentence summary*, including author and title.

Sentence Summary: Kelly Green focuses on the problem of disorientation in the first year of retirement, then describes the adjustments retirees have made to solve the problem, including modification of personal attitudes and spending habits ("How to Survive the First Year").

Student Sample 2

> In "Reshaping Retirement Scenarios and Options" (*The Futurist*, 2004), Moynach and Worsley performed a two year study called "The Tomorrow Project," in which they analyzed the changing conditions of retirement. Based on interviews, consultations, and focus groups, they formulate new approaches for structuring individual retirement plans and state pension programs that will better serve the people of Great Britain."

Follow-up: Instruct student to underline the most important sentence, then write a *one-sentence summary*, including author, title and source.

Sentence Summary: "In the Tomorrow Project," Moynagh and Worsley formulate new approaches for structuring individual retirement plans (*The Futurist* 2004)

The Review of Criticism

Now that you have raided the library shelves for the relevant "holdings," you have the beginnings of a "working bibliography"—and just that. The search for relevant intelligence has just begun, however. The length of any given research project determines how exhaustive your bibliography must be. But in any paper, whether short or long, whether a 5-7 page midterm or a 200 page dissertation, a *review of the relevant "intelligence" (or criticism)* is an effective rhetorical strategy. It not only gives your reader the scholarly context of your discussion, but by establishing your credibility on the subject goes a long way to fulfilling the primary goal of your writing: to persuade (or otherwise heighten the effect upon) the reader. In writing the 8-12 page undergraduate research paper, this "review of the relevant criticism" can be handled in a few sentences or in a short paragraph: one that serves as a springboard into your own argument. It provides the initial impetus to your argument, which then unfolds in critical counterpoint (or as a substantive addition) to this critical "conversation."

The idea is simple.

Find the critical conversation(s) occurring in the subject area, and shoulder your way into one: by finding a gap in the debate, an angle that has not been sufficiently considered, or considered at all. In response to the criticism, the writer should be thinking "Yeah, but what about this or that . . . ?" After this review of the "relevant intelligence" you may be in a position to write, by way of introducing your own thesis, as follows:

> "Although many critics have noted the significance of _____ in so-and-so's work, none to my knowledge have commented on _____.

Note: the "to my knowledge" gives the writer-researcher the necessary critical cover, in case your search has failed to turn up a critic who has weighed-in on your focus.

The Review of Criticism/Rhetorical Strategies

Several rhetorical strategies can be effective in composing this critical review, or this summary of the *critical conversation*, on a focused subject. Following are some syntactical arrangements you may find useful for concisely, yet substantively, summarizing your own sources:

- "Several critical cruxes have driven the scholarly debate on _____."

- "While critics such as _____ have argued X, others such as _____ have argued Y."
- "None to my knowledge, however, has argued Z."
- "Initially, critics argued X. More recently, however, criticism has focused on Y."
- "The critical tradition on _____ can be divided into several camps."
- "Published commentary on. . . Joyce tended to become either exclusively laudatory or exclusively derogatory, depending on which position the reviewer took in the politics of art" (Kershner 248);
- "For the last quarter century Proustian criticism has been dominated by the theories of Lacan and Derrida. . . . Reading against the grain of an earlier modern tradition, these provocative postmodern interpretations have sparked lively debate. . . . "(Brown 7).
- "The single most influential essay on *Portrait* of the time, Hugh Kenner's 'The Portrait in Perspective'. . . . sets the terms for the arguments of other critics" (Kershner 250).
- "Diverse interpretations characterize the critical debate over _____."
- "_____'s essay touches on. . . while _____ contends that. . . . "
- "_____, on the other hand, points out that. . . ."
- "Finally, _____ stresses that . . ."
- "These critics stress that . . . ."
- "_____ , on the other hand, protested that . . . ."
- "_____, by contrast, hailed . . . ."
- "Meanwhile, many critics were less concerned with Joyce's moral stance . . . than with the internal complexities of the work . . . . True to the formalist assumptions of the New Critics, Tindall looks at . . . . " (Kershner 251).

- "Studies of the novel's structure include. . . "(252).
- "The natural course of Joyce criticism was altered forever by the publication of Richard Ellmann's magisterial biography *James Joyce* in 1959. . . . which spurred interest in Joyce's composition process" (253).
- "The 1970's saw the impact of. . . a variety of Continental critical approaches" (253).
- "A renewed interest in Marxist criticism. . . (and in socially and politically based criticism in general) led to a new critical distance. . . " (253).

These rhetorical structures, moreover, can be used for summarizing sources across disciplines, in science as well as in literature.

Writing-to-Learn/The Review of Criticism

- In journal, write a one-sentence summary of your four most relevant sources.
- Share in group.
- "Recorder" makes a master list.
- "Reporter" shares with class.
- At home, make a one-sentence summary for every work you quote.
- Rank these sources from weakest to strongest or according to the sequence they are used in your paper.
- Combine your summary sentences into a paragraph. This will be the rough draft for your "review of the relevant criticism."
- Share in group.
- Volunteers share aloud with class.
- Type up a pre-final edit and hand in for grade.
- Incorporate instructor's feedback into a final edit, and add to your research portfolio.
- Instruct students to write one-sentence summaries of their four most relevant sources, and record them in a journal entry.

Review of Criticism/Conclusion: The ability to briefly assess an article or book's contribution to a "conversation" in a single sentence is a useful rhetorical strategy, not only for concretely developing your argument in the body, but for setting it up with a concise review of the criticism in the paper's introduction. The purpose of this critical part of an argumentative paper is threefold: first, to provide some scholarly *context* for the reader, as well as the *framework* for your own argument, to which it serves as a *springboard;* second, it sets the *scholarly tone* of the discussion, analysis, or argument; and finally, it establishes the writer's *credibility* at the outset by evidencing the extent to which his or her interpretations are informed by substantive research. Thus, the critical review helps the writer take that first, significant step toward achieving the paper's overall purpose: persuasion of the reader/audience. It gives the reader a sense of the "conversation" to date on the critical cruxes under discussion. Finally, if the writer has done the labor of finding, assessing, and distilling the relevant intelligence on a focused subject, then why not "get the most mileage of out of it," by commencing your paper with a brief summary of the cogent sources?

Naturally, the scope of this review of criticism depends on the scope of the writing project. For an academic paper (8-12 pages, 12-15 pages, 15-20 pages), the writer should devote no more than several sentences or a paragraph to the critical review, focusing on those sources most relevant to the paper's focus. To further economize space, these works can be referenced in footnotes/end notes. If properly handled, the review of criticism will not only accomplish these objectives, but function as a springboard into the writer's own inquiry/argument.

Scholarly tone. Comprehension. Credibility. Rhetorical momentum.

These are strengths well worth the investment in time and effort necessary to craft a brief review of the most relevant sources to your focus.

If done well, the final result might look something like this:

> "Historically, the reduction of the sophistic project to the exercise of a particular style (Murphy, *History* 8), to an exhibition of personal power by the orator (Kennedy, *Rhetoric* 16-17), or at worst to the amoral manipulation of an audience (Sedgewick) indicates the powerful influence on histories of rhetoric by Plato and Aristotle" (Jarratt, *Rereading the Sophists* xvi).

Research and Reader Response: Writing in the Margins

Writing a paper is not something that happens *after* the research is done. It occurs *before, during, and after* the research phase. The research and writing process is not sequential and linear, but concomitant and recursive. Thus, begin writing your paper *while* you are researching it, in the margins of the sources you are reading. In other words, while reading the relevant sources, you are already developing your own "reading" of them, or their relevance to your thesis—in writing, by writing in reaction to what you read. This *talking-back-to-texts* activity is essential for two reasons: it concretely develops your thesis, while simultaneously developing a strong, argumentative "voice" in your writing. These are two *must-have* assets for an effective argumentative paper.

Having located the sources of your working bibliography, the arduous task of reading them commences in earnest. At this stage of the journey it is useful to emulate the work ethic and field tactics of the prospector, paleontologist, geologist, archeologist, or anthropologist, by pouring through this mass of critical words with a fine tooth comb, sifting the various "sites" for those bits and fragments of relevant intelligence that will find their way into your paper by virtue of their relevance to your thesis. Your critical eye is your geologist's magnifying glass. The work is time-consuming, even tedious at times, and requires the tireless determination of a detective searching for decisive clues in the field. No one can do this work for you. It is a solitary, challenging, yet richly rewarding labor. The pay-off comes when you are able to clinch a point you have made, a claim you have asserted, with a quote that aptly, if not perfectly, reinforces it—that seems almost custom made for your claim. The relationship between claim and supporting evidence is one of natural kinship. For every claim there must be at least one piece of supporting evidence; it is your task as a researcher to find it. Having found it, it is your challenge as a writer to integrate it into your text in juxtaposition to the claim it supports, then further develop its significance for your thesis, by explicating its meta-textual, hidden, between-the-lines, meanings.

These quotes, once found, extracted, and integrated into your text, add concrete development to your logic, credence to your argument, and substance to your thesis. The reward for all the effort is a final edit in which other voices blend and unite with your own in a compelling, perhaps novel, development of a significant focus: one that brings a fresh perspective to an old debate, that takes it in a new direction, or that completely reverses the "received wisdom" of previous interpretations. All it requires is a keen eye, a commitment to the task, and a faith that you WILL find what you are seeking—that you too will experience that EUREKA moment when you discover the precise quote for which you have been searching, that exactly supports a point you have made in your argument—as well as other, unforeseen quotes, whose relevant intelligence takes your argument in directions as fresh and productive as they are serendipitous.

With your sources (and pen) in hand, begin reading with a hungry vigilance. As you read the course texts you have purchased, the sources or the sources you have Photocopied, "talk back" to the text in its margins, as outlined in Chapter One. As does the scientist in the field, develop a labeling system for retrieval of "relevant intelligence," for the division and classification of the empirical evidence you discover in the multiple sites of other texts: "Q" for quote; "Intro"/"Concl" for quotes to use at the beginning or end of your paper; check-marks beside passages you want to quote;

minus signs to indicate things the critic attacks; "lim" to indicate a limitation or flaw in the argument you want to respond to; question marks and written questions beside passages you want to interrogate in your paper; "def" for an apt definition of a key term you want to include in your paper, etc. Most importantly of all, in the margins scribble the ideas you want to develop in your paper, for these "graftings" comprise the beginnings of your own text.

In this process, the acts of reading and writing go hand in hand. As you respond to the text, you have in effect already begun writing your paper. The act of critical reading is a springboard into critical writing. Search for the gaps in reasoning, the things not said, the contradictions, the assumptions unexamined, the counter-arguments ignored or missed, the limitations of an argument, or the avenues of further development that were overlooked, the associations with other passages or other texts, with your own experience. Question, argue, and engage the text in a *conversation* of your own making, in ink, in the margins. Your own "reading" has its humble origins in this marginal "back-talk." Why not capture a little of this intellectual lightning in a bottle as it occurs, with pen in hand.

Writing to Learn: Writing in the Margins

- Write in the margins of a source you have photocopied, responding to 20 pages of text, using your own system of symbols to facilitate the retrieval process.
- Photocopy a page and share in group, talking them through your marginalia, de-coding your symbols.
- Add-on at home, making this a regular part of your research process.

Integrating Quotes into a Research Paper

How can the academic writer effectively integrate quoted material into his/her own text? There are several effective rhetorical strategies for accomplishing this "splice" between another's words and your own: five, in fact—each of which I will model. First, it should be noted that no source should be quoted unless that quote warrants inclusion in your paper, unless it relates directly to your thesis, or to some claim you have made in support of your thesis—and just as importantly, unless it adds significance to your argument. Sans this relevant significance, this scholarly "gravitas," if you will, a quote has no business being quoted. To warrant inclusion in your paper, a quote must be both relevant and substantive.

If there are diverse ways to get the reader's attention and to develop your thesis, so too are there a number of means by which to integrate quoted material into your own text. What you are seeking is a seamless splice of another's words and your own, so as not to disrupt the continuity of your writing.

A Three-Step Process: Weaving any quote into your text involves three steps, as follows:

- Introduce the quote in your own words.
- Reproduce the quote (word-for-word, including its punctuation); followed by the page number in parenthesis, and a period.
- Explicate (develop) the significance or implications of the quote; "read between the lines" as it were, for your reader.

This last is the most important part of the quoting process and, alas, the one most often ignored by novice academic writers—an unfortunate omission because such explication of a quote also adds depth of analysis to your paper, reinforces the "play of mind," which you want to introduce into your paper at every opportunity.

When first quoting from a given source (book, article, website) you must also mention the author's full name and the full title of the work, either in your introduction of the quote, or in the parenthetical reference to it. If using APA style, you must also include the year of publication in the parenthetical reference, between author's name and page number (Brown, 2002, 65). (See citation guidelines for MLA, APA, and Chicago Style.)

Caution: A Pitfall

Your paper can have *NO free-standing quotes*. What is a free-standing quote? Just what its name implies: a quote that is written as a sentence by itself, that is not introduced or coupled to your own words. Every quote *MUST* be integrated into your words. Of the many conventions that govern academic writing, this is one of the conventions most commonly broken by first-year writers (as well as by their upper-division peers).

Example of Free-Standing Quote (FSQ)

> "The effort to reform education should include unmasking biased practices such as tracking. 'Students not classified as middle class are often viewed as academically inferior. Most of these students are greatly harmed by such expectations'" (Chin, Gollnick 65).

Revised Version

> As Chin and Gollnick assert, "Students not classified as middle class. . . " (65).

Five Rhetorical Choices

There are five ways to handle your introduction/attribution of a quote in order to achieve that seamless splice between another's words and your own:

- Author attribution, followed by the quote (A-Q)
- Quote, followed by author attribution (Q-A)
- Quote, interrupted by author attribution (Q-A-Q)
- A "key word" quote
- A block quote

1. Author/Quote

By far, the most common and useful of these is the first: the author introduction, followed by the quote. I've found a simple introductory clause (with multiple variations on it) to be the most effective means of integrating a quote into my own text, as follows:

Example 1

As Goethe states, "Q" (p).

Note: Quotes are generally introduced in the present tense (the "eternal present") whether the author of the quote is living or not. This is a rule which (like most rules) can be broken. As a rule, however, do not flip-flop between tenses when quoting: consistency is a virtue here. The problem with using "As Goethe states," for every quote you introduce is that it quickly becomes redundant, giving a "broken-record" quality to your syntax, or word choice—or lack thereof. Some effective variations of this introductory clause can be quickly achieved, however, by merely substituting other words for "states," as follows: observes, asserts, affirms, avers, argues, writes, attests, notes, etc. (see list page 65). Instead of introducing a quote with this clause, you can introduce it with a sentence, as long as you take care to change the punctuation from a comma to a colon:

Example 1

Goethe's observations are worth noting: " . . . . . . " ( ).

Example 2

Goethe's words are instructive: " . . . . . " ( ).

Again, it is important to note that introducing a quote with a clause requires a comma, whereas introducing a quote with a complete sentence necessitates a colon.

A Few Simple Rules

- The first time you cite a source, you must include the author's full name and the full title in your introductory clause or in the parenthetical page reference. Thereafter, one word abbreviations are used as necessary.
- Titles of books are italicized (or underlined); titles of articles, chapters are framed by quotes.

- When quoting, the comma always comes before the quotation marks. No exceptions.
- The end quotation marks are always followed by the parenthetical page reference, followed by the period: ". . . ." (14).
- To indicate words omitted from the end of a quote, include three elipses, as follows: . . . "(14).
- With respect to the parenthetical page reference, only the number appears within it:

Incorrect Examples: (page 14); (page # 14) (page 14).

Correct Examples: (14), (14-16).

- If you've mentioned the author's name in your introductory clause, do not repeat it in the parenthetical page reference. As long as you continue to quote from the same source, there is no need to cite the author's name with every quote.
- However, if you begin citing from a second source and then return to your original source, you must include the author's last name, either in your introductory words or in the parenthetical page reference: ". . . " (Smith 14).

2. Quote/Author

A simple variation of this rhetorical strategy involves reversing the order. Begin with the quote and end with the author attribution, placing a comma between.

Example 1

"Nothing is more terrible than ignorance in action," asserts Goethe.

Example 2

"The eternal feminine draws us on," Goethe observes. Note: again, note the presence of the comma before the end quotes.

3. Quote-Author-Quote

Yet another effective variation is to break a quote in two, inserting the author attribution in between. This requires a quote that lends itself to this division, which works best with parallel constructions or with sentences that require a "felt sense" for breaking them in two, as follows:

Example 1
"Just trust yourself," Goethe advises, "then you will know how to live" ( ).

Example 2
"Law is mighty," Goethe asserts, "mightier necessity" ( ).

Variety, as with life, is the spice of effective writing. Rhetorical variation will heighten the effect on your reader, so that at no point will he or she be victimized by words (or phrases) repeated ad nauseam as the result of a creeping redundancy, or "deja vu" writing.

4. The Key Word Quote

Another option for splicing quoted text into your own is to quote a few key words instead of the entire quote. This not only adds variety to your rhetoric, but brevity, a useful device if your paper is fast approaching the maximum page limit of the assignment. So instead of the following:

Example 1
As Goethe confides, "I call architecture frozen music" ( ).

You might write,

Example 2
Goethe compares architecture to "frozen music" ( ).

Example 3
Goethe asserts that necessity is "mightier" than law ( ).

Student Example 1
According to Freire, the biggest downfall of educational systems and institutions is the "banking" style of teaching in which information is "deposited" in the student by teachers with no real interaction or discussion (71).

Key word quotes, if properly handled, are not only an effective space-saving device, but are one of the most effective means of achieving a seamless splice between another's words and your own. Further, they add emphasis to your writing by highlighting the main point of a source.

5. The Block Quote

A final means of adding not only substance but also variety to your argument is to incorporate a passage or two from another text (4+ lines or longer). Like quoting itself, this should not be over-done. As when quoting a sentence, the block quote must be introduced (or attributed) with a few words of your own. If it is introduced with a clause, that clause must end in a comma; if it is introduced with a complete sentence, however, that sentence must end in a colon. This is the only place in your paper where you have the option of *double or single spacing*, as long as every block quote is spaced the same.

Whether single- or double-spaced, the block quote is governed by a few simple conventions, as follows:

- It must be 4+ lines (four lines or longer) to warrant being blocked.
- It begins one double-space down from the words that introduce it.
- Similarly, it is followed by one double space when your own text resumes.
- The entire block quote takes a double tab on the left—in other words, it is indented one additional tab from your paragraph break.
- On the right hand side, however, it takes the same margin as the rest of your paper—in other words, it is aligned with your own text.
- A block quote takes *no quotation marks*, except when you are quoting dialogue or a quote-within-a-quote: then it takes the normal double quotation marks.

- The end of a block quote is also different, inasmuch as the period comes *before* the parenthesis instead of after it. Do NOT ask me why.

Student Sample

Isocrates also credits social discourse, specifically language, with a central role in determining action and thought. Anticipating postmodernism and the linguistic turn, Isocrates writes:

> Because there has been implanted in us the power to persuade each other and to make clear to each other whatever we desire, not only have we escaped the life of wild beasts, but we have come together and founded cities and made laws and invented arts; and generally speaking, there is no institution devised by man which the power of speech has not helped us establish. ("Antidosis" 327)

Ellipses: Editing Block Quotes

The purpose of ellipses (…) or (….) is to achieve emphasis and clarity by eliminating unnecessary words—i.e., words unrelated to the relationship you are establishing between your text and the quoted text. Ellipses enable you to compact a long, wordy quote into a smaller space. Ellipses also enable you to edit a block quote for relevance, emphasis, clarity, and conciseness: all desirable virtues in academic writing. As with quoting in general, and with quoting lengthy passages in particular, this rhetorical device should not be overdone. A block quote in which the omitted words outnumber the quoted words calls the writer's credibility (and worse, his or her integrity) into question. The reader begins to wonder what has been left out, and if the meaning has been changed because words are now appearing out of context. Therefore, use ellipses economically and ethically, in a way that in no way alters the meaning of the writer's words.

This said, there are passages where words can be deleted without altering the writer's meaning. This can heighten the effect on the reader by creating a more succinct quote (even as it may save you critical space in a paper that is approaching its word/page limit). The rules for using ellipses are simple, as follows:

- Use three dots (. . .) to signify *words* that have been deleted from a quote.
- Use four dots (. . . .) to indicate *sentences* that have been deleted from a quote.

Note: Whether using three or four dots, leave a space between each dot.

Note: During the final-edit phase of your paper, it is necessary to double check the accuracy of every quote. This includes double-checking the accuracy of authors you have quoted who have used ellipses to delete words/sentences, by checking these against the original to make sure the quoted version has not altered the meaning of the original by taking it out of context. If this is the case, you have three choices: restore the original, drop the quote from your paper, or add a qualifier in which you call into question the quoting author's credibility for taking a quote out of context. By double-checking a quote with ellipses against the original, you may discover new means of adding critical development to your thesis.

Writing-to-Learn: Integrating and Explicating Quotes

- In your journal, quote a source with proper attribution, integrating it into your own words, mentioning the author's complete name and the full title of the source;
- Integrate four more quotes into your own words, using the four strategies modeled in this chapter, as follows:
    1. "quote," author
    2. author, "quote,"
    3. "quote," author, "quote."
    4. Key-word quote.
- Integrate a "block quote" into your text, following the relevant conventions.

- Share in group, making any necessary corrections.
- Volunteers share one example of each with class.
- In your journal, record a quote from a library source you checked out, with proper page reference. Free-write a response to this quote by "reading between the lines," developing its relevance to your thesis, explicating its significance or hidden meanings, its weaknesses, contradictions, or limitations, its associations with other passages or text, etc.
- Share in group.
- In journal, add on at home, recording and explicating every quote in a given source that supports your thesis (focus).

This essential activity adds concrete development and "voice" to your argumentative writing. It adds depth of analysis and "play of mind" (yours): two of the greatest assets of academic writing, which heighten the credibility and persuasive impact of your argument. When combined with the marginalia you have written in course texts and photocopied sources, these reader-response free-writes constitute the initial draft of your paper. While reading, you are discovering the material for developing your thesis. Though it will end as a free-standing document, your paper begins in the margins of another's words, or on an empty page, under the quoted "heading" of another's words. These two forms of reader-response in the research moment evidence the efficacy of writing, not just after the research moment, but during and before it. They model a vision of academic discourse in which the invention, research, and writing of a paper are not part of a linear sequence, but of a concomitant process in which all are occurring simultaneously and continuously—at least until the very final phases, where invention, discovery and research of necessity give way to arrangement, editing, and "finishing." This approach to academic writing envisions the research process as a dynamic moment that affords abundant, practical, and useful opportunities for writing—in which the moment of writing-to-discover and writing-to-develop is not deferred until after all the relevant material has been read, but while it is being read. In this model of academic writing, the search for knowledge and the making of knowledge occur simultaneously, thanks to the synergy of the reading and writing moments.

The Works Cited Page

(For reinforcement, refer to the samples on page 81 and 89.) There are several technical, formatting conventions to follow in crafting the Works Cited page, as follows:

- Center the words, Works Cited, at the top of the page.
- Thereafter, the entire page is *double-spaced*, beginning with the words "Works Cited" to the final period of the final entry. In other words, entries are double-spaced within AND between.
- Individual entries are listed alphabetically by author's last name.
- The works cited page is paginated consecutively from the first page of your text.
- Each source-entry has three categories of information, each separated by a period, as follows: Author. Title. Publishing information.
- For books, there are three sub-categories of information in the publisher category, as follows: City: Publisher, Year.
- A book entry is punctuated, as follows:

    Hemingway, Ernest. *The Sun Also Rises*. New York: Scribner's, 1926.

    1. A comma separates Last name, First name.
    2. The book title is *italicized*. A colon separates book title: subtitle. *Style: Ten Lessons in Clarity and Grace.*
    3. A colon separates City: Publisher.
    4. A comma separates Publisher, Year.
    5. Periods separate the three main categories: Author. Title. Publishing Info.
    6. And a period follows the year. Thus, every entry (book or article) has at least three periods.

Works Cited

Barr, Bob. "Liberal Media Adored Gun-control Marchers." Insight on the News 5 June 2000: 44. ProQuest. Lemieux Lib., Seattle U. 15 Aug. 2001 <http://proquest.umi.com>.

Barry-Buchanan, Malik. "More Rules + More Security=Feelings of Safety." Alternet.org 16 Aug. 2001 <http://alternet.org/print.html?StoryID=9623>.

Del Prete, Tony. "Unsafe Schools: Perception or Reality." Professional School Counseling 3 (200): 375-76.

Ferraraccio, Michael. "Metal Detectors in the Public Schools: fourth amendment concerns." Journal of Law and Education 28 (1999): 209-29.

Gress, Jon. "School Violence: How to Stop the Crime of Today's Youth." Gecko-the Student Server 5 May 2000. 16 Aug. 2001 <http://gecko.gc.maricopa.edu/-jtgress/argue2.htm>.

Harrington-Lueker, Donna. "Metal Detectors." American School Board Journal 179.5 (1992): 26-27.

Lee, Venture. "Detectors Alarm some Students." Said & Done. Urban Journalism Workshop. Summer 2000. 16 Aug. 2001 <http://ujw.philly.com/2000/detector.htm.

Lindsey. "Re: School Security." Online posting. 23 Oct. 1999. Juvenile Information Network. 16 Aug. 2001 <http://ww.juvenilenet.org/messages/27.html>.

- Author, Title: Subtitle, City, and Publisher are all written as they appear on the title page.
    1. If the name as it appears on the title page includes an initial, a Jr., or roman numerals (III), this is how it is written on the works cited page.

2. Delete abbreviations like "Inc." and "Co." from the publisher's name, as follows:

   Macmillan (not Macmillan & Co.); Random House (not Random House Inc.)

3. The year is taken from the copyright page, located after the @ copyright symbol.

- The first line of each entry is flush left; subsequent lines are indented one tab.

   Batholomae, David."Inventing the University." *When A Writer Can't Write*. Edited by Mike Rose. New York: *Guilford*, 1985.

- An article is punctuated as follows:

   Allen, R.E. "Law and Justice in Plato's *Crito*." *Journal of Philosophy* 69 (1972): 557-67.

   1. A comma separates Last name, First name.
   2. The article title is bracketed by quotes.
   3. The *four* sub-categories of the publishing information are punctuated as follows: *Journal name* in italics, followed by volume number, followed by date in parenthesis, followed by inclusive page numbers. A colon is inserted between the (date) and the page numbers, as follows: 1998: 21-27. Periods separate Author. Title. Publishing Information—with a period after the page numbers.

- Multiple entries by the same author are handled as follows:

   Graff, Gerald. "Teach the Conflicts." *South Atlantic Quarterly* 89 (1990): 51-67--. "In Defense of Teaching the Conflicts" In *Teaching the Conflicts. . . . Culture Wars*. William E. Cain. New York: Garland, (1994).

   1. Three dashes and a period (---.) take the place of the author's name.
   2. The author of the book in which the article appeared is listed as indicated above (William E. Cain).

      This applies as well to *editors of collections*, preceded by an "Edited by," as follows:

> Bizzell, Patricia. "Marxist Ideas in Composition Studies." In *Contending With Words . . . Postmodern Era.* Edited by Patricia Harkin and John Schilb. New York: MLA, 1991. 52-68.

- For works by two or more authors, the first is listed alphabetically by last name, followed by the remaining co-authors, as follows:

> Ashcroft, Bill, Gareth Griffiths and Helen Tiffin. *The Post-Colonial Studies Reader.* New York: Routledge, 1995.

- List electronic sources from the Web, as follows:

> Kimihiko, Yishii and Tonagai Yauhide. "Water Content . . . Pesticide Standards." *Journal of Health Science* 50.2 (2004): 142-47. June, 2005. Http://www.jstage.jst go.jp/browse/jhs/50/2/_contents//h.

1. The format is identical through the first three categories of Author. Title. Publishing Information.
2. After this information, merely record the month and year when the web site was visited, followed by the complete web address.

The Research Presentation/Colloquium

As a capstone to your research project you will give a brief presentation highlighting the genesis of your project, which will include the following:

- A brief introduction on the origin of your project, of your interest in its particular focus.
- The central research question.
- A research "action plan," describing your strategies for finding and retrieving sources.
- A reflective narrative highlighting the "ups" and "downs," the successes and frustrations, of the research process.
- A description of the system you developed for organizing the data.

- A description of your "information retrieval and extraction strategies," of what worked best or worst, and any "pitfalls" in the process.
- An anecdote of your worst experience in the entire process.
- Identification of any gaps in your research base that you were unable to fill.
- A brief description of future avenues of research to be pursued were you to continue this project.
- A brief description of how you assessed the credibility or worthiness of your sources.
- A brief enumeration of any lessons learned, things you would do differently with the benefit of hindsight.

Writing-to-Learn: Research Presentation

- Working from your research portfolio, cobble together the journal entries related to these aspects of your research project into a draft for your research presentation.
- Share in group.
- Rewrite, incorporating any useful group feedback.
- Type up in format suitable for a presentation (triple space, two-sentence paragraphs, etc.)
- Hand in typed draft after presentation for a grade.

Conclusion/Summary

This chapter is designed to develop a "cluster of abilities" in the academic researcher, as follows:

- Develop effective strategies for identifying and retrieving information.
- Develop effective strategies for evaluating/assessing the information.
- Develop effective strategies for integrating the information into your own text.

- Develop effective strategies for documenting the sources of the information.
- Develop effective strategies for disseminating the information to your peers;
- Develop effective strategies for extracting the information.

This "cluster of research abilities," when combined with the invention and discovery strategies modeled in chapter one, comprise the contents of a "rhetorical tool kit" that enhance the prospects of meeting with a high degree of success in your academic writing career. Moreover, many of these strategies have "real world" value in the career marketplace across professions, many of which privilege the ability to find, assess, synthesize, and disseminate information. Proficiency in these communication skills will pay dividends not only in your academic career, but in the real world of "applied learning" beyond the classroom.

Additional Sources/Subject

Education

Resources in Education (REI): Provides abstracts of 1k new, unpublished educational materials from ERIC (Educational Resources Index Center), including conference papers, seminar reports, reviews of research, etc. Accessed by headings from Thesaurus of Descriptors (section on Indexing and Retrieval).

Current Index to Journals in Education: Indexes published material in 750 journals related to educational fields. Both an abstracting and indexing service; also a catalogue. A product of ERIC. Available on-line. Contains articles in chronological order, Subject/Author indexes, and a Table of Contents of Indexed Journals. Useful for teachers of literature and composition. Superior to R.E.I. because the contents have been published.

Education Index: Lists articles in 350 education-related periodicals and other sources. An Author/Subject Index, that is available on-line. Alphabetized by author/subject. Easier to search than ERIC.

English Studies/Literary Criticism: General

Year's Work in English Studies: An annotated serial bibliography of English and U.S. authors, with the emphasis on British authors and criticism. 800+ periodicals searched. Annotated volumes have an author-as-subject index. Periodicals indexed by headings. Useful for identifying trends, for quick searches, for developing a bibliographic review of the relevant criticism. Less current than MLA IB.

New Cambridge Bibliography of English Literature (NCBEL)

Oxford Companion to English Literature

Oxford Companion to American Literature

Annals of English Literature (1475-1950)

Prentice Hall Guide to English Literature

Twentieth Century Literary Criticism (TCLC)

Contemporary Literary Criticism (CLC)

Essay and General Literature Index

Biographical Sources

Dictionary of Literary Biography (DLB)

Dictionary of American Biography

Biography Index (BI)

Poetry

Columbia Granger's Index to Poetry

American and English Poetry: A Guide to the Criticism

Guide to American Poetry Explication

Poetry Criticism

Novels

The American Novel: A Checklist of...Criticism... Since 1789

The Contemporary Novel: A Checklist . . . on the British and American Novel Since 1945

English Novel Explication

Short Stories

Twentieth-Century Short Story Explication

Short Story Criticism

Critical Survey of Short Fiction

Drama

A Bibliography of the English Printed Drama to the Restoration

Critical Survey of Drama

Drama Criticism Index

Victorian Literature

Wellesley Index To Victorian Periodicals: An index to articles in 43 selected Victorian periodicals, including 12k writers of the 19th century. Volume B contains an Index of Contributing Authors, plus a list of contributing articles in alphabetical order. More detailed than Poole's Index, while accessing a smaller core of periodicals. No poetry.

Renaissance

Literature of the Renaissance

Medieval

International Medieval Bibliography

*International Guide to Medie*val Studies

Social Sciences

International Encyclopedia of Social Sciences

History
Literary History of the US (LHUS)
American Bibliography

Philosophy
The Encyclopedia of Philosophy

Works Cited Format

General Format for a Book

Author. "Chapter or Part of Book, " *Title of Book: Subtitle*. Ed. (editor). # edition. #vols. Series. City: Publisher, Year. Pages used. Annotation.

[Multiple books by the same author may use three hyphens (or an em-dash) after the first entry.]

Derrida, Jacques. "Plato's Pharmacy." *Dissemination*. Trans. Barbara Johnson. Chicago: University of Chicago Press, 1981. 61-171.

—. *Politics of Friendship*. Trans. George Collins. London: Verso, 1997.

—. "Psyche: Invention of the Other" (excerpt). Trans. Catherine Porter. *Acts of Literature*. Ed. Derek Attridge. New York: Routledge, 1992. 310-43.

General Format for a Newspaper

Author. "Title of Article." *Name of Newspaper* [City] Day Month Year [Edition]. Inclusive page numbers.

Anderson, Kendall. "Archives Combed for Cherokee Ties." *Dallas Morning News* 3 July 1994: 49A, 52a.

General Format for a Magazine

Author. "Title of Article." *Name of Magazine* Day Month Year: Inclusive page numbers.

"Which Cars Are Safest in a Crash." *Consumer Reports* Apr. 1993: 199, 202.

Gleiberman, Owen. "Crazy for You." Rev. of *Benny and Joon*, dir. Jeremiah Chechick. *Entertainment Weekly* 23 Apr. 1993: 36-37.

General Format for a Scholarly or Professional Journal

Author. "Title of Article." *Name of Journal* Series Number Volume Number (Date): Inclusive page numbers.

Melchior, Bonnie. "Teaching *Paradise Lost:* The Unfortunate Fall." *College Literature* 14.1 (Winter 1987): 76-84.

Incorporating Documented Information

Introducing Quotations
Susanne Langer responded, "The vulgarization of art is the surest symptom of ethic decline" (310),

W. H. Auden remarked that "a culture is no better than its woods" (271).

Altering Quotations

Introduce and Indent long quotations:
Donna Haraway sees primatology as a narrative practice:
> Primatology is about the life history of a taxonomic order that includes people. Especially western people produce stories about primates while simultaneously telling stories about the relations of nature and culture, animal and human, body and mind, origin and future. Indeed, from the start, in the mid-eighteenth century, the primate order has been built on tales about these dualisms and their scientific resolution. (Primate 5)

Brackets provide clarification of pronouns when the original context has been removed or provide identification for pre-existing errors:

> The words of Thomas Jefferson offer us a philosophy for detente: "We must therefore . . . hold them [the British] as we hold the rest of mankind, enemies in war, in peace friends."

> Teaching can be frustrating to the point that Mark Twain once described: "I'll learn [sic] him or kill him."

> Henley's poem "Invictus" reminds us that with self-determination we can be "the master[s] of [our] fate."

When you omit material from a quote, use an ellipsis (three spaced periods with a space before and after each point):

> Susan B. Anthony inspires us to take action when she reminds us that "cautious, careful people . . . never can bring about reform."

Understanding always takes place with reference to the future, a point on which Heidegger is quite explicit:

> If the term "understanding" is taken in a way which is primordially existential, *it means to be projecting towards a potentiality-for-Being for the sake of which any Dasein exists.* . . . The future makes ontologically possible an entity which is in such a way that it exists understandingly in its potentiality-for-Being. (385; italics in original)

Citations in the Text

Note: Consult Bedford Chapter 53 (584-613) for detailed explanations and examples of MLA documentation format. You will be expected to conform to this standard on all research-based assignments. You will be penalized on final drafts for failure to conform to MLA format. Failure to properly cite and credit sources may constitute plagiarism.

Example 1:
The most memorable lines in *The Grapes of Wrath* are spoken by Tom Joad as he takes up the work of the preacher Casy after the latter was beaten to death for standing up for the unity and dignity of the farm laborers:

> Whenever they's a fight so hungry people can eat, I'll be there. Whenever they's a cop beatin' up a guy, I'll be there. . . . I'll be in the way guys yell when they're mad an'—I'll be in the way kids laugh when they're hungry an' they know supper's ready. An' when our folks eat the stuff they raise an' live in the houses they build—why, I'll be there. (Steinbeck 537)

Example 2:
John Steinbeck uses the rhetorical figure called epistrophe when he repeats the phrase "I'll be there" in Tom Joad's famous speech in *The Grapes of Wrath* (537).

Example 3:
Henry Petroski, a professor of civil engineering at Duke University, delves into the area of industrial design in his book *The Evolution of Useful Things*. Fresh from the success of his previous work, *The Pencil*, Petroski now tackles the paper clip, the four-tined fork, the zipper, the pop-top aluminum can, McDonald's polystyrene-foam clamshell containers (discontinued for environmental reasons in 1990), and other artifacts from commercial America, like Post-It notes, the Bostitch stapler, and plastic garbage bags.

Example 4:
Since 1991, there have been 50 percent more mentions of Elvis sightings in the *New York Times* ("Harper's Index" 11).

Example 5:
The "not-but" construction, also known as antithesis, is illustrated by Shakespeare's "Not that I loved Caesar less, but that I loved Rome more" (qtd. in Booth and Gregory 114).

Example 6:
David Feldman takes up the perplexing question "How do they decide where to put thumbnotches in dictionaries?" (*Penguins* 167-68).

MLA Style Guide

Style Guide is based on the *MLA Handbook for Writers of Research Papers*. This is a guide to the most frequently used entries. If you need additional help, there are copies of the handbook available on Reserve, at the Circulation Desk (Reserve Call # LB 2369 G53 2003). For further help citing electronic references see:

www.bedfordstmartins.com/online/citex.html
University Libraries www.library.univ.edu

Revised, August 2004

Citing Books

Book—single author
Works Cited
Wilson, Frank R. The Hand: How Its Use Shapes the Brain, Language, and Human Culture. New York: Pantheon, 1998.
In text:
(Wilson 10)

Book—two or more authors
Works Cited
Eggins, Suzanne, and Diane Slade. Analyzing Casual Conversation. London: Cassell, 1997.
In text
(Eggins and Slade 304)

Book—a translation
Works Cited
Murasaki, Shikibu. The Tale of Genji. Trans. Edward G. Seidensticker. New York: Knopf, 1976.
In text
(Murasaki 25)

Work in an Anthology or Compilation
Works Cited
Allende, Isabel. "Toad's Mouth." Trans. Margaret Sayers Peden. A Hammock beneath the Mangoes: Stories from Latin America. Ed. Thomas Colchie. New York: Plume, 1992. 83–88.
In text
(Allende 83)

Citing Journals

Journal Article
Works Cited
Barthelme, Frederick. "Architecture." <u>Kansas Quarterly</u> 13.3-(1981):77-80.
In text
(Barthelme 79)

Article from a Newspaper
Works Cited
Lohr, Steve. "Now Playing: Babes in Cyberspace." <u>New York Times</u> 3 Apr. 1998, late ed.: C1+.
In text
(Lohr C1)

Anonymous Article
Works Cited
"The Decade of the Spy." <u>Newsweek</u> 7 Mar. 1994: 26-27.
In text
("Decade" 26)

Article in a Microform collection of Articles
Works Cited
Chapman, Dan. "Panel could Help Protect Children." <u>Winston-Salem Journal</u> 14 Jan. 1990: 14. <u>Newsbank: Welfare and Social Problems</u> 12 (1990): fiche 1. grids A8-11.
In text
(Chapman A9)

Citing Web Materials

An Article in an online scholarly journal
Works Cited
Calabrese, Michael. "Between Despair and Ecstasy: Marco Polo's Life of the Buddha." <u>Exemplaria</u> 9.1 (1997). 22 June 1998 <http://web.english.ufl.edu/english/exemplaira/calaz.htm>.
In text
(Calabrese)

An Article in an online newspaper or newswire
Works Cited
"Endangered Species Act Upheld." <u>AP Online</u> 22 June 1998. 22 June 1998 <http://www.nytimes.com/aponline/w/AP-Court-

Endangered-Species.html>.
In text
("Endangered" par.2)

Personal Site
Works Cited
Dawe, James. Jane Austen Page. 15 Sept. 1998
    <http://nyquist.ee.ualberta.ca/~dawe/austen.html>.
In text
(Dawe)

Professional Site
Works Cited
Romance Languages and Literatures Home Page. 1 Jan. 1997. Dept.
    of Romance Langs. and Lits., U of Chicago. 8 July 1998 <http://
    humanities.uchicago.edu/romance/>.
In text
(Romance Languages)

Journal article from an online service to which a library subscribes
Works Cited
Tolson, Nancy. "Making Books Available: The Role of Early Libraries,
    Librarians, and Booksellers in the Promotion of African American
    Children's Literature." African American Review 32 (1998): 9-16.
    JSTOR. 1 Oct. 2002 <http://www.jstor.org/search>.
In text
(Tolson 10)

Chicago Manual of Style Guide

This Style Guide is based on the *Chicago Manual of Style*. It is a guide to the most frequently used entries. If you need additional help, there are copies of the manual available on Reserve, at the Circulation Desk, and in Reference (Call# Rdf Z 253 U69 2003). For further help see www.libs.uga.edu/ref/chicago.html.

University Libraries www.library.univ.edu
Revised, January 2005

Citing Books

Book—single author
Works Cited
Blackfoot, Emery. *Chance Encounters*. Boston: Press, 1987.
Footnote
    1. Emery Blackfoot, *Chance Encounters* (Boston: Press, 1987), 10.

Book—two authors
Works Cited
Unwin, Liam P., and Joseph Galloway. *Peace in Ireland*. Boston: Press, 1990.
Footnote
    1. Liam P. Unwin and Joseph Galloway, *Peace in Ireland* (Boston: Press, 1990), 24.

Book—edited
Works Cited
Tortelli, Anthony B., ed. *Sociology Approaching the Twenty-first Century*. Los Angeles: Peter and Sons, 1991.
Footnote
    1. Anthony B. Tortelli, ed., *Sociology Approaching the Twenty-first Century* (Los Angeles: Peter and Sons, 1991), 35.

Book—Translation
Works Cited
Giankakos, Peter, and William Poweska, trans. *Studies of Transformation*. Buffalo. N.Y.: Touser and Blinkem, 1991.
Footnote
    1. Peter Gianakakos and William Poweska, trans. *Studies of Transformation* (Buffalo, N.Y.: Touser and Blinkem, 1991), 61.

Book—Chapter
Works Cited

Phibbs, Brendan. "Herrlisheim: Diary of a Battle." Chap. 7 in *The Other Side of Time: A Combat Surgeon*. Chicago: University of Chicago Press, 1987.

Footnote

    1. Brendan Phibbs, "Herrlisheim: Diary of a Battle," in *The Other Side of Time: A Combat Surgeon*. (Chicago: University of Chicago Press, 1987), 117-63.

Citing Journals
Journal article
Works Cited

Robertson, Noel. "The Dorian Migration and Corinthian Ritual." *Classical Philology* 75 (1980): 1-22.

Footnote

    1. Noel Robertson, "The Dorian Migration and Corinthian Ritual," *Classical Philology* 75 (1980): 17, 19-20.

Newspaper Article
Works Cited 7

Finnonian, Albert. "Robert, Moses, Master Builder, Is Dead at 92." *New York Times,* July 30, 1981, Midwest edition.

Footnote

    1. Albert Finnonian, "Robert, Moses, Master Builder, Is Dead at 92," *New York Times*, July 30, 1981, Midwest edition.

Book Reviews
Works Cited

Spitzer, Steven. Review of *The Limits of Law Enforcement*, by Hans Zeisel. *American Journal of Sociology* 91 (November 1985):726-29.

Footnote

    1. Steven Spitzer, Review of *The Limits of Law Enforcement*, by Hans Zeisel, *American Journal of Sociology* 91 (November 1985):726-29.

Movie Reviews
Works Cited

Kauffmann, Stanley. "Turbulent Lives." Review of *A Dry White Season* (MGM movie). *New Republic*, October 9, 1989: 24-25.

Footnote

    1. Stanley Kauffmann, "Turbulent Lives." Review of *A Dry White*

Season (MGM movie), *New Republic*, October 9, 1989: 24-25.

Citing Web Materials

Article from an electronic journal—accessed through a database
Works Cited
Thomas, Trevor M. "Wales: Land of Mines." *Geographical Review,* 46 no. 1 (1956): 59-81, http://.jstor.org.
Footnote
    1. Trevor M Thomas, "Wales: Land of Mines," *Geographical Review* 46, no. 1 (1956): 59-81, http://.jstor.org.

Newspaper article from an electronic database
Works Cited
Satel, Sally. "OxyContin Half-truths Can Cause Suffering." *USA Today*, October 27, 2003, final edition, Lexis-Nexis. http://www.lexis-nexis.com/universe.
Footnote
    1. Sally Satel, "OxyContin Half-truths Can Cause Suffering," *USA Today*. October 27, 2003, final edition, Lexis-Nexis, http://www.lexis-nexis.com/universe.

Online Government publication
Works Cited
U.S. Census Bureau. "Health Insurance coverage Status and Type of coverage by Sex Race and Hispanic Origin, 1987 to 1999." Health Insurance Historical Table 1, 2000. http://www.census.gov/hhes/hlthins/historic/hihistt1.html.
Footnote
    1. U.S. Census Bureau, "Health Insurance coverage Status and Type of coverage by Sex Race and Hispanic Origin, 1987 to 1999," Health Insurance Historical Table 1, 2000, http://www.census.gov/hhes/hlthins/historic/hihistt1.html.

Professional site
Works Cited
The Bahá'ís of the United States. "History," *The Bahá'í Faith*. http://www.us.bahai.org/history/index.html.
Footnote
    1. The Bahá'ís of the United States, "History," *The Bahá'í Faith*, http://www.us.bahai.org/history/index.html.

APA Style Guide

APA Style Guide is based on the *Publication Manual of the American Psychological Association*. This is a guide to the 3 most frequently used entries. If you need additional help, there are copies of the manual available on Reserve, at the Circulation Desk, and in Reference (Call # BF76.7 P83 2001). For further help citing electronic references see:
www.bedfordstmartins.com/online/citex.html

University Libraries www.library.univ.edu
Revised, September 14, 2004

Citing Books

Book
Works Cited
Mitchell, T.R., & Larson, J.R., Jr. (1987). *People in organizations: An introduction to organizational behavior* (3rd ed.). New York: McGraw-Hill.

In text
(Mitchell & Larson, 1987)

Book—edited
Works Cited
Gibbs, J.T., & Huang, L. N. (Eds.). (1991). *Children of color: Psychological interventions with minority youth*. San Francisco: Jossey-Bass.

In text
(Gibbs & Huang, 1991)

Book—no author or editor
Works Cited
Merriam-Webster's collegiate dictionary (10th ed.). (1993). Springfield, MA: Merriam-Webster.

In text
(Merriam-Webster's collegiate dictionary, 1993)

Book—Article or chapter in an edited book
Works Cited
Massaro, D. (1992). Broadening the domain of the fuzzy logical model of perception. In H.L. Pick Jr., P. Vanden Broek, & D.C. Knill (Eds.), *Cognition: conceptual and methodological issues* (pp. 51-84). Washington, DC: American Psychological Association.

In text
(Massaro, 1992)

Citing Journals & ERIC Documents

Journal article
Works Cited
Klimoski, R., & Palmer, S. (1993). The ADA and the hiring process in organizations. *Consulting Psychology Journal: Practice and Research, 45(2)*, 10-36.

In text
(Klimoski & Palmer, 1993)

Journal Article—more than six authors
Works Cited
Wolchik, S.A., et al. (2000). An experimental evaluation of theory-based mother and mother-child programs for children of divorce. *Journal of Consulting and Clinical Psychology, 68*, 843-856.

In text
(Wolchik, et al., 2000)

Newspaper Article–No author
Works Cited
New drug appears to sharply cut risk of death from heat failure. (1993, July 15). *The Washington Post*, p. A12.

In text
("New Drug", 1993)

ERIC document
Works Cited
Mead, J.V. (1992). *Looking at old photographs: Investigating the teacher tales that novice teachers bring with them* (Report No. NCRTL–RR-92-4). East Lansing, MI: National Center for Research on Teacher Learning. (ERIC Document Reproduction Service No. ED346082).

In text
(Mead, 1992)

Citing Web Materials

Document available on a website
Works Cited

Chou, L., McClintock, R., Moretti, F., & Nix, D.H. (1993). *Technology and education: New wine in new bottles: Choosing pasts and imaging educational futures.* Retrieved August 24, 2000, from Columbia University, Institute for Learning Technologies Web site: http://www.ilt.comlumbia.edu/publications/papers/newwinel.html.

In text
(Chou, McClintock, Moretti, & Nix, 1993)

Electronic copy of a journal, retrieved from a database
Works Cited
Borman, W.C., Hanson, M.A., Oppler, S.H., Pulakos, E.D., & White, L.A. (1993). Role of early supervisory experience in supervisor performance. *Journal of Applied Psychology, 78,* 443-449. Retrieved October 23, 2000, from PsycARTICLES database.
In text
(Borman, Hanson, Oppler, Pulakos, & White, 1993)

Online Newspaper article
Works Cited
Hilts, P.J. (1999, February 16). In forecasting their emotions, most people flunk out. *New York Times.* Retrieved November 21, 2000, from http://www.nytimes.com.
In text
(Hilts, 1999)

Online Government publication
Works Cited
U.S. General Accounting Office. (1997, February). *Telemedicine: Federal strategy is needed to guide investments* (Publication No. GAO/NSAID/HEHS-97—67). Retrieved September 15, 2000, from General Accounting Office Reports Online via GPOI Access: http://www.access.gpo.gov/su_docs/aces/aces160.shtml?/gao/index.html.
In text
(U.S. General Accounting Office, 1997)

Research Paper
Outside Sources—Worksheet #1 *TCLC*

Due—Next Class

Assignment: Go to the library, locate the following source-books and answer the respective questions regarding Jack London, *Call of the Wild*, and *White Fang*.

Note: For your term paper–final exam you will be required to cite (quote) at least two outside sources with proper attribution as to author, title page #. You will also be expected to include a list of *works cited* at the end of your paper.

Twentieth Century Literary Criticism (TCLC) light brown, ask librarian to locate.

Instructions: Locate this collection of reference books which list *excerpts* from reviews of books published in the 20th century. It is an excellent source for quotes, and for surveys of book reviews.

1. In the back of *Volume 41*, you will find an author-index, arranged alphabetically by author's last name (always a good place to begin a search). Find the entry for *London*. After his name you will find a cross-reference to other volumes in which you may find reviews of London's works. In what *3 volumes* will you find such reviews?

2. Taking the volumes in numerical order (beginning with the lowest number first) find the section on *London*. Again the entries are listed in alphabetical order by author's *last name*.

   a. Does the biographical sketch come at the beginning or end of the section?

   b. In the biographical sketch of London it tells you from whom he took his name. Who was this person?

   c. How many books did he publish in his career?

   d. What were some other occupations he held before he became a working writer?

   e. What did he disguise himself as while gathering material for a book about the slums of London?

3. Locate the review by Van Wyck Brooks, published in 1952. What does he say about Buck and the law "kill or be killed, eat or be eaten?"

4. According to Van Wyck, how was London like Buck?

5. Are these reviews arranged in alphabetical or chronological order?

6. Locate the essay by Maxwell Geismer, published in 1953. What comparison does he draw between human beings and the dogs, as portrayed in *Call of the Wild*?

7. What does Geismer say about the "theory of racial instinct" as it is developed in *Call of the Wild*?

8. What does he write about Buck, Spitz, and Freud?

9. Geismer writes that *White Fang* and *Call of the Wild* deal with contrasting impulses: what are these impulses, according to Geismer?

10. According to Geismer what spoils the ending of *White Fang*?

11. Locate the essay published in 1903 by J. Steward Doubleday. What does he say about the philosophy of "survival of the fittest" as it's portrayed in *Call of the Wild*?

12. Locate the 1956 essay by Charles Chiles Walcutt. What does he have to say about the "hairy man" and the "wolves who Buck hears howling at night"?

CHAPTER 2

Resources Worksheet #2

The following questions pertain to *CLC* (Contemporary Literary Criticism). Light brown set of books, to left of *TCLC*.

1. In the back index to volume 41 of *TCLC* look up the entry for Golding, William. (Entries are arranged alphabetically by author's last name) In which volumes of CLC does the index say you can find information on Golding?

2. In what year was he born? Which country is he from? **Take vol.** 3 of CLC off the shelf and look up Golding.

3. According to the first review by Kenneth Rexroth "All _____ novels are rigged." This quote was taken from an article titled "_____ _____" published by the magazine, _____ _____(give title of magazine.)

4. According to the review by David Anderson, "*Lord of the Flies* is a complex version of the story of _____, the man whose _____ _____ failed and who murdered his _____."

5. According to Mr. Anderson, "What we have in *Lord of the Flies* is not moral _____, but moral_____."

6. The title of Mr. Anderson's article is "_____."

7. According to Mr. Anderson, how has regression occurred on a gigantic scale in the world from which the rescue boat comes?

8. Why does he say *Lord of the Flies* fits the definition of a Fable?

9. He goes on to state that "Golding has compelled us to acknowledge that there is in each of us a _____ _____."

Replace Vol. 3 and take Vol. 2 off the shelf and look up Golding.

10. According to Steven Marcus, Golding began his career as a _____.

11. According to James Gindin, "Each of Golding's first 3 novels is governed by a massive _____." The title of the article in which this quote appears is "_____."

12. According to Frank Keruda, why is *Lord of the Flies* a "comforting book."

Worksheet #3

The following questions pertain to *DAB* (Dictionary of American Biography):

1. The entry for Jack London can be found between pages_____. In vol. _____(give #).

2. According to the biographical sketch of London, he was born in the city of _____. His father was a _____.

3. "Almost all his writing. . . has to do with one motif (theme)—the _____."

4. "Toward the end of his life he made several pleasure trips to _____."

The following questions pertain to *Biography Index* (BI). (Index Table):

5. Look up the entry for Golding, William. According to this entry John Clifford Mortimer published an interview with William Golding in a book called _____. The interview appears on pages _____ of the book.

6. Look up the entry for Jack London. Stanford University Press published something by Jack London in 1988 which was 1657 pages long. What was it? The work *did / did not* (choose one) include illustrations.

The following questions pertain to *British Writers* (blue & red cover—opposite wall from *TCLC*):

7. The entry for Golding is found on pages _____.

8. "By the time Golding was 7 he began to connect the darkness with the _____. From them he learned _____ & _____."

The following questions pertain to *DLB* (Dictionary of Literary Biography):

9. In what year was *Lord of the Flies* first published? How old was Golding at the time? At the time he working as an unknown _____.

10. According to Golding, "There's really no point in writing a novel unless you do _____ _____" (page 120).

11. The manuscript was rejected by how many publishers before it was finally accepted?

12. According to Golding, "The theme is an attempt to trace the _____ of society back to the _____ of nature."

CHAPTER THREE

The Introduction: Rhetorical Strategies and the First Moment of the Product

Preview

This chapter models rhetorical strategies related to the Introduction of a thesis-driven paper, as follows:

- Introducing a *thesis*
- Stating a thesis
- Previewing the *criteria* by which the thesis will be *developed*

Having generated sufficient information to concretely develop a thesis (statement of opinion) through the invention and discovery, free-write and rewrite, research and development phases of the writing process, the search for relevant intelligence, for all practical purposes, ends. At this point the emphasis shifts from discovery to arrangement, from concrete development to writing for clarity and correctness, from the process to the product of writing, from "writing to learn" to "learning to write," as Fulwiler observes—though not absolutely. However, invention and discovery should continue right up until the pre-final edit, allowing for those last minute epiphanies or discoveries that sometimes only occur after the writer/researcher's grasp of an issue's or text's complexities has gained a depth and comprehensiveness that generates fresh insights. Thus, while not absolute, the shift in emphasis from process to product is absolutely necessary at this "moment" of the writing journey.

The Purpose

In order to write an effective introduction to an essay, it helps to understand the *purpose* of an introduction. Indeed, the primary parts of an academic paper (introduction, body, and conclusion) each have a distinct purpose. It is, therefore, useful at each stage of this intellectual enterprise to know what the purpose of your writing is at any given point.

What then is the purpose of an introduction?

Simply stated, it is threefold: first, to arouse the reader's interest; second, to state WHAT you will prove or argue; and third, to state HOW will you prove or argue it. At the outset of your essay, the reader wants (and needs) to know two things: what is the FOCUS of the paper and HOW you will develop that focus. In addition, they want their interest to be aroused. Consequently, there are three elements to an effective introductory paragraph, each of which fulfills one of these three purposes:

- the *attention getter*
- the *thesis statement*
- and the *criteria of development*

The 1st Moment of the Introduction: Attention-Getters

Before stating your thesis (or what you will argue), it is desirable to arouse the reader's interest and/or provide some valuable context or background to the focus of your inquiry. There are several effective ways to do this.

- The rhetorical question
- The quote
- The definition
- The graphic fact
- The "scene setter"

- And the review of criticism, background summary, or historical overview

These rhetorical strategies can also be used effectively in combination; as follows

- A quote, followed by a question that in turn sets up a thesis
- A quote, followed by a scene setter, that sets up the central research question, which the thesis then answers
- A graphic fact or definition that introduces the central research question, which the thesis subsequently answers
- A quote, which sets up the central research question, which in turn sets up a review of the criticism, which sets up your thesis

I would like to discuss each of these *attention getters* in turn, modeling effective strategies for their practical use.

1. The Central Question(s)

Beginning an essay with a question (or series of questions) is effective for two reasons: It gains the reader's attention and simultaneously focuses the inquiry. A rhetorical question is not only an effective attention getter, but one that is easily found, insofar as it is often provided by the instructor, and is (as often as not) embedded in the essay writing assignment. If not provided by the instructor, then this attention-getting question should already have been articulated by the writer as the first step of the inquiry process—in the form of the *central question(s) for research or inquiry*. There is yet a third virtue to beginning with a rhetorical question, which complements, if not supersedes, its first two virtues: it is a springboard into your argument and interpretation in general, and into your thesis in particular—a working version of which can be quickly crafted in answer to this central research question(s).

Examples
- Which is more important: a person's right to privacy or the public's right to know?

- Should gangsta' rap lyrics be censored for their racist, misogynistic, and nihilistic content?
- Should national parks be devoted to preservation or recreation?
- Is Shakespeare's *Titus Andronicus* the work of a fledgling or accomplished dramatist?
- What are the causes and effects of binge drinking on college campuses? And, more importantly, what should be done to solve the problem?

Writing-to-Learn: The Attention-Getting Question

- In your journal, craft a question or series of question related to your paper's focus?
- Share in group.
- In group, revise, incorporating any useful suggestions for improving it (editing for clarity and emphasis).
- "Recorder" compiles a master list of group's questions.
- "Reporter" shares one with the class.

Follow-Up

- As a group, craft separate questions for a writer's particular focus.
- Share.
- Rank from weakest to strongest;
- Revise, combining effective elements of different questions, or writing an attention getter that uses several of these questions.
- "Recorder" writes down the final draft of the attention-getting question(s).
- "Reporter" shares with class.

2. The Opening Quote

There are two ways to effectively handle a quote that launches an essay, as follows:

- As a free-standing quote, single-spaced under the title, indented with a double tab on the left, followed by a double-dash and the author's name, followed by the page number; or
- As the first words of the essay, properly introduced by your own words, with proper attribution of author, title, and parenthetical page reference.

There are numerous advantages to beginning an essay with an apt quote, as follows:

- It gets the reader's attention (the more so if highlighted under the title).
- It sets the *scholarly tone* of the essay.
- It establishes the writer's *credibility* as a researcher on the subject.
- And it announces to the reader the *focus* of the inquiry.

More than ample reward for the effort required. In short, an apt quote at the beginning of an essay adds a nice rhetorical touch, giving the writing that level of "finish" that satisfies. Moreover, if the writer has done his or her "homework," has gone to the trouble of digging up usable quotes during the research "moment," then why not reap the reward of your efforts by further highlighting an elegant or "spot-on" quote. Opening quotes are like well-wrought titles: they catch the reader's eye. More importantly, they commence the process of persuasion at the very outset of the essay, winning a measure of admiration in the very first "moment" of writing. I am vigilant for the opening and closing quotes to an essay throughout the research process, identifying them when discovered with a simple labeling system ("intro"/"concl'). They give an essay the emphatic beginning and climactic assessment it deserves. Finally, if selected properly, these opening and closing quotes function like scholarly bookends to a writer's collected thoughts, giving a sense of finish to the essay and of satisfaction to the reader. A small, but important, contribution to the scholarly aesthetic of the essay—especially if it is a quote that warrants its place under the title or in the first sentence your write.

The Free-Standing Quote (under the title):

Example 1 (my own)

Title: *Metaphor and Composition: Problems, Practices, & Implications*

Quote: "The rogue never hazards a metaphor."
—Dr. Johnson (on Jonathon Swift)

lst Sent. All too often in the composition classroom, creativity is separated from analysis, the imagination from the intellect. . . .

Student Sample 1: (from paper, "*Toward Process: The Rejection of the Teacher-Centered Classroom*")

> "A writer is not so much someone who has something to say, as he is someone who has found a process that will bring about new things he would not have thought of if he had not started to say them."
>
> —William Stafford (Poet)

Student Sample 2: First sentence of essay.

> "There is no conceivable way," observes homicide detective Smith, "that a federal ban on handguns could save a single life or prevent a single injury."

Student Sample 3: (from "The Freshman Crunch: Dealing with the Pressures of College")

> "Stress is the unbridled source of evil that haunts the day-to-day life of every college freshman." These are the sentiments of junior Angus Guberman, a seasoned veteran of college life.

Student Sample 4:

> I find that writers are more than people who write; they are, as William Stafford says, "people who have fallen in love with a certain process that instructs their lives."

Writing-to-Learn: The Attention-Getting Quote

- Retrieve a quote from your research or course readings that relates to your own writing focus. You may, if you choose, use a quote from your reader-response journal, already culled from your research/course readings.
- Make a journal entry, using this quote as a *free-standing attention getter*, under a working title for your paper.
- Make an entry in which you begin your paper with this quote, integrating it into your own words, with proper attribution.
- Share in group; group comments on its effectiveness.
- "Recorder" compiles master list of group quotes.
- "Reporter" selects one to share with class.

Follow-Up

- At home, in journal, go back through the texts your have read as part of your research, labeling the best candidates for this attention-getting quote. I use a simple symbol for identifying and retrieving these quotes, which I place in the margin beside them: "QQQ/ Intro" or "QQQ/Open."
- Photocopy a page of text showing these quotes and their respective marginal symbol.
- Share in group.

3. The Definitional Beginning

Another effective means of beginning a paper is with the definition of a key word. If, for example, you are writing a paper debating whether women should be allowed in combat, an introduction that begins with a definition of "combat" can be an effective attention-getter. Similarly, if you are writing a paper on whether "date rape" is really "rape," beginning with a definition of "rape" and/or "date rape" can be an effective opening. Like the rhetorical question, the definitional beginning is effective for several reasons: it not only sets the scholarly tone and announces the subject of the paper, but by defining what is (and just as importantly, what is not) meant by a key term in the argument, it establishes the argumentative parameters of the debate. This adds clarity to your argument by circumventing misunderstandings grounded in false assumptions about the meaning of "combat" or "rape." The definitional beginning establishes whether "combat" will be broadly or narrowly defined, in traditional or contemporary terms, as "hand-to-hand" or "push-button": an important distinction in arguing whether the "battlefield" is or is not a fit place for women, and whether a woman has as much right to serve, fight, or die for her country as a man.

Example 1 (student sample)

> "Clown: a clumsy, boorish or incompetent person; a performer who entertains, as in a circus, by antics, jokes, or tricks; a jester; a person who constantly plays the fool. In Shakespeare's *Twelfth Night*, Feste, the clown does not seem to comply with these standard definitions."

A fine enough introduction, yet one that could be made even more effective with a few simple upgrades to the thesis, as follows: begin the second sentence with "Feste;" upgrade the verb "does not seem to comply " to "subverts;" and heighten the diction from "with standard definitions" to "stereotypic comedic conventions."

Revised Version

> "**Feste,** the clown in Shakespeare's *Twelfth Night*, **subverts** stereotypic comedic conventions of this stock character."

The definitional sentence that sets up this thesis is fine, as is.

Example 2

> "Discover: to make known or visible. . . to obtain sight or knowledge of for the first time. . . also, find out" (*Webster's* 222). The "discovery phase" is a critical part of any legal

case. Yet, traditionally, this phase of the academic writing process has been overlooked or marginalized in the writing classroom.

Definitional beginnings not only reinforce the scholarly credentials of the arguer, but introduce the focus of the paper: in this case, an argument touting the efficacies of writing-to-discover thought. The following definitional beginning achieves the same two objectives in a paper on *Women in Combat*:

Example 3

> "Combat: conflict, warfare, battle, close combat—fight, oppose, contend, struggle against."
>
> —Webster's, 160

Writing-to-Learn: the Attention-Getting Definition

- In your journal, make an entry in which you list the most important "key terms" that will inform your argument, and which your research has uncovered.
- Choose one, and write a definition for it, giving proper attribution to your source.
- Share in group.
- "Recorder" compiles a master list.
- "Reporter" selects one to share with class.

Follow-Up

- In journal, write definitions for the rest of the "key terms" on your list.
- Rank in order of importance or order in which you will use them.
- Share list in group.

4. The Graphic Fact

Yet another effective attention-getter is the "graphic fact." By this,

I mean a fact that packs some punch, that hopefully produces a visceral response in the reader. It gets the reader's attention in the same way a loud noise would (a car's backfire, a thunderclap, a fire-alarm). It says, effectively, "Wake up and pay attention." The "graphic fact" is most effectively packaged as a short, declarative statement. A few student samples:

- 30,000 gun-related homicides are committed every year in America.
- In 1992, handguns were used in 931,000 violent crimes—a 21% increase over the 1991 total.
- "Of the 174,000 active Marines, 9300 are women," all of whom are "gender segregated" from their male counterparts throughout their training at Paris Island.
- Of the hottest average annual temperatures ever recorded on earth, the top five have occurred in the last ten years.
- The average American contributes 15,000 lbs of carbon dioxide to the atmosphere every year.

A simple statement of graphic fact at the outset of your argument realizes the a priori objective of your paper: to heighten the effect upon the reader. This should be the goal of your words at every phase of the writing process, from introduction to conclusion, from "attention getter" to "clincher."

Writing-to-Learn: The Attention Getting Fact

- In your journal, make an entry in which you list the five most significant facts your research has uncovered.
- Chose one, and write an opening sentence to your paper, using this fact.
- Share in group.
- "Recorder" compiles a master list.
- "Reporter" shares with class.

CHAPTER 3   **115**

Follow-Up
- Make a journal-entry in which you write an attention-getting sentence for each of these facts.

5. The "Scene Setter"

A critical review or historical summary are not the only ways to "set the scene" of an academic inquiry. There is yet another way to provide some critical context: the hypothetical "scene-setter." This consists of a brief, hypothetical dramatization of your attitude/opinion on a given topic. The scene-setter is an effective attention getter because in a paper that is going to rely largely on quotes, facts, logic, and/or personal experience to develop its thesis, it allows you to infuse a little color and sensory detail into it, and a little "color" can go a long way in an argument that relies primarily on concrete development to make its case. Additionally, the scene setter, by dramatically and succinctly stating your thesis on a controversial issue, makes effective use of one of Aristotle's three argumentative "appeals": the appeal to pathos. This fulfills, at the outset, one of the goals of your argumentative writing: to heighten the effect on the reader—wherever and whenever possible. The operative words here are "little" and "brief." Again, we're talking 2-3 sentences in a paper that will range from 5-15 pages Following is an example of an effective scene-setter:

Example: Women in Combat

> 6'5", 220 pound pfc John Chase lies gravely wounded between combatants in the Iraqi desert. 5'4", 105 pound Jessica Lewis heroically dashes to his side, exposing herself to enemy fire. She tries to lift and throw her fallen comrade over her shoulder, but staggers under the weight and falls to a knee. A round of .50 caliber bullets stitches her body, and both drop to the ground, her blood coagulating in the desert dust with that of her brother. Despite the advent of push-button warfare, the battlefield is still a place requiring physical strength and hand-to-hand combat, and therefore no place for "the fairer sex."

The brief "scene-setter" not only arouses the reader's interest with the dramatic verbs and sensory detail, but also sets up the paper's thesis. It is like a movie trailer, enabling the writer to infuse some style and color into a paper that hereafter will privilege substance and concreteness. Again, a little "color" like this will go a long way in an academic paper. The pitfall to avoid is getting carried away with the make-believe dramatization to the point of violating the principle of part-to-whole. I have read student scene-setters that went on for two pages, which would be fine in a fiction-writing course, but which offend the sense of proportionality in an argumentative essay.

Student Sample: (from paper, "Stress and the College Freshman")

> "As I walk into the bathroom, I see one of my dorm mates leaning against the wall sobbing. Her silent tears clearly express an unbearable pain. When I ask her what the problem is, she replies "I feel nauseous and my head is pounding." As I continue questioning her about her condition, the tears flow in excess while she rambles on of all her worries about schoolwork and lack of sleep. I feel her pain, but cannot do anything, except remind her that she's experiencing a typical symptom of stress.
>
> Stress seems to be a daily occurrence in the busy lives of young college students."

Writing-to-Learn: The Attention-Getting Scene Setter

- In your journal, free-write a scene setter on a given topic (private ownership of guns, women in combat, college binge drinking, same-sex marriage etc) that hypothetically, yet concisely dramatizes your opinion (thesis);
- Share in group;
- Volunteers share aloud with class;
- In journals, make an entry in which you free-write a role-playing "scene-setter," writing about gun control from the perspective of a victim or victim's relative, or on the women-in-combat

issue from the point of view of the opposite gender, a relative, or the enemy.
- Share in group.

Follow-Up: Combining Attention Getters

- In your journal, make an entry in which you write an extended attention getter, in which you use at least three of the following in combination: quote, question(s), definition, graphic fact, and scene-setter.
- Share in group.
- Group provides feedback on strengths and weaknesses of the attention getter, offering suggestions for improving it.
- Volunteers share aloud with class.
- At home, in journal, revise, incorporating any useful suggestions from the group's feedback.

Bridge-Work

Having effectively gotten the reader's attention, you are now in a position to (succinctly and forcefully) state your opinion on the issue. The whole purpose of the attention-getter is to set up your thesis. Having raised the question, you now answer it. Having introduced the focus of your inquiry, you now state your position on it. How to effectively do this? As with every other phase of the academic writing process, there are several practical strategies you can use to craft an effective thesis: one that emphatically and concisely announces your position—which you will then spend the rest of your paper developing or proving.

The 2nd Moment of the Introduction: The Thesis Statement

Having garnered the readers' attention (and hopefully aroused their interest), it now falls to the writer to concisely and emphatically tell the reader what he or she will argue (or endeavor to prove) in the essay—in a single sentence. This is manifestly a high-stakes sentence (perhaps the most important in the entire paper), as it states the opinion to which all subsequent content will relate, (whether facts, stats, or quotes; personal experience, logic, or refutation of the counter arguments) and which all subsequent content must develop. The thesis states the opinion from which every other word is descended. An essay, in a very real sense, develops genealogically from this first, primal "attitude." Anything unrelated to it has no place in the essay. If every word in an essay is relational, the thesis is the parent back to which they all refer, to which they are all related. The thesis is, therefore, the master referent of the entire essay.

A writer's task is made easier by the fact that a thesis statement needn't be eloquent. What it must be, however, is concise and emphatic. This section models several rhetorical strategies for writing thesis statements that possess the two critical virtues: that are as forceful, as they are succinct.

The thesis is not the place to mince words. It is the moment, par excellence, when writing must be attitudinal—when the writer writes with a strong attitude. Consequently, a short, emphatic thesis is generally more effective than a long and wordy one—though this is a rule, which like any rule of academic writing, can be broken selectively, for effect. The thesis should leave absolutely no doubt about the writer's position, which must be asserted with a strong attitude. To achieve this, a thesis requires one or two "forceful" words.

Writing-to-Learn: The Problematic Thesis 1

Problematic Example: "In my opinion, outlawing handguns is a bad idea."

The effect here is weakened by the wordiness and the ho-hum diction (word-choice). A simple edit and diction upgrade will solve the problem, as follows:

- Delete the "in my opinion."

- Upgrade the verbs "outlawing" and "is" to more forceful or dramatic verbs, "banning" and "violates."
- Begin with this more dramatic verb, "banning."
- Appeal to the reader's logos or reason, by giving this thesis a legal context.

Effective Example: Banning private ownership of handguns violates Americans' constitutional rights.

Analysis: Upgrading the verbs "outlawing" and "is" to "banning" and "violates" adds dramatic emphasis to the attitude asserted, as does beginning the thesis with a dramatic verb ("banning"). Situating the opinion within the framework of "constitutional rights" further strengthens it, by giving it a solid legal foundation. The "in my opinion" can easily be deleted as redundant: a thesis is, by definition, an opinion. If it were a fact, there would be no room for argument.

In short, it's much more effective to wallop the reader upside the head with a rhetorical two-by-four, than to flagellate the reader with a limp spaghetti noodle of a thesis that wanders all over the page in a vain search for strength. Beginning with a strong verb ("banning") and reinforcing it with a second strong verb ("violates) is an effective means to an emphatic thesis.

Writing-to-Learn: The Problematic Thesis 2

Another sequence with which to arrive at an effective thesis is as follows:
- Answer the central question raised in your attention getter.
- Begin your answer with "in my opinion."
- Delete the "in my opinion."
- Finally, upgrade a few key words for scholarly emphasis.

Example 1
- Question: "Should women be allowed in combat?"

- Answer: "In my opinion, women should be allowed in combat.
- Edited version: "Women should be allowed in combat"
- Upgraded final version: "Women have the same right to fight and die for their country as men," or conversely, "The battlefield is no place for a woman."

Example 2

- Question: Should Gangsta' rap lyrics be censored or banned?
- Answer: "In my opinion, Gangsta' rap lyrics should not be censored or banned."
- Edited version: "Gangsta' rap lyrics should not be censored or banned."
- Upgraded version: "Censoring Gangsta' rap lyrics is an unconstitutional infringement of freedom of expression."

Assessment: The upgraded diction ("unconstitutional infringement"), the front-loaded verb ("censoring") and the phrase "freedom of expression," add emphasis, scholarly tone, and legal weight, respectively, to this thesis. Any one of these virtues will heighten the effect of your thesis on the reader. In tandem, that effect is significantly compounded.

Example 3

- Question: On the issue of government surveillance of private phone conversations, which is more important: national security or an individual's right to privacy?
- Answer: In my opinion, protecting individual privacy is more important than safe-guarding national security.
- Edited Version: Protecting individual privacy is more important than safe-guarding national security.
- Upgraded version: Safe-guarding national security is a misguided imperative if in that very attempt the Constitution is destroyed.

Assessment: Again, with a few simple upgrades, for emphasis, scholarly tone, and legal merit, this is now an effective thesis. The verb has not only been upgraded from "protecting" to "safe-guarding," but front-loaded for dramatic emphasis. The diction has been similarly upgraded from "is more important" to "a misguided imperative," heightening the scholarly tone and forcefulness of the language, while the reference to the Constitution heightens the appeal to logos. Emphasis, scholarly tone, legal weight: the three graces of an effective thesis statement.

Writing-to-Learn: Upgrading a Thesis 1

- In journal, make an entry in which you answer your central research question, beginning with "in my opinion."
- Practice using the strategies modeled to upgrade the thesis, as follows:
    1. Delete the "in my opinion."
    2. Upgrade the verb.
    3. Front-load the verb.
    4. Add a second dramatic verb.
    5. Upgrade another key phrase for scholarly tone.
    6. Give your opinion a constitutional context if you can.
- Share in group.
- Group provides feedback, noting strengths and weaknesses of each thesis, ways to upgrade it.
- "Recorder" compiles a mast list of theses.
- "Reporter' selects one to share with class.
- At home, revise thesis, incorporating any useful feedback from group.

Writing-to-Learn: Problematic Thesis 3

Yet another useful means for crafting an effective thesis statement is to adopt the following rhetorical strategy: "Although some critics think X, I think Y."

Example 1: "Although some people believe (date rape) isn't really (rape), I believe it does even more violence to the victim—and should be punished accordingly."

Example 2: "Although some critics assert that Shakespeare's *Titus Androncius* is the work of an amateur playwright, I believe the play is early evidence of his dramatic genius."

Example 3: Although some critics contend that the persuasive essay is a useless relic of the past, I believe fluency in persuasive communication equips students for academic and professional success, given its ubiquity across disciplines and professions.

Writing-to-Learn: Upgrading a Thesis 2

- At home, in your journal make an entry in which you craft a thesis using the "although some think, I think," strategy.
- Share in group.
- Volunteers share aloud with class.

Follow-up

- At home, in journal, make an entry in which you combine your extended attention-getter and your thesis statement.
- Share in group.
- Group responds, noting strengths and weaknesses of the attention getter + thesis.
- Volunteers share with class.
- At home, revise, incorporating useful feedback from group.

The 3rd Moment of the Introduction: The Criteria of Development

Now that you have effectively gained the reader's attention and stated what you will argue in your paper, it only remains to preview for the reader how that argument will be made—to state the several criteria by which the thesis (opinion) will be developed. If the thesis statement tells the reader *what* you will argue, the next sentence or two previews *how* you will argue your position. This part of the introduction, consequently, previews the arrangement of your entire argument (essay). If you will argue your criteria from weakest to strongest, it makes sense to preview them in your introduction in the same order.

This final "moment" of the introduction fulfills a critical function insofar as much of the paper's clarity and the reader's comprehension of the argument flows from it. In tandem, the "what" and the "how" of an introduction provide the reader with an argumentative road-map that fosters both clarity and comprehension, that "imprints" the course of the argument on the reader's mind, by previewing both its focus and development. This rhetorical "imprint" of an argument is particularly helpful to the reader in longer papers (12 pages +).

By previewing in the introduction an argument's destination and development, the writer naturally sacrifices a measure of suspense. However, while suspense may be a desirable, if not essential, virtue for a mystery writer, it is trumped in the academic essay by a different virtue: clarity. The persuasive writer's tactics are, therefore, similar to the lawyer's—who previews to the jury both the verdict being sought and the means that will be used to reach it. The case then unfolds as a methodical and climactic march of evidence that concludes, as it began: with the verdict (thesis). This rhetorical strategy not only previews the arrangement of your argument, but serves as a transition into the first phase of it: from the focus of your argument to the development of that focus.

Example

- Attention Getter: Should women be allowed in combat?
- Thesis: Although many people believe women should be allowed in combat, I believe that the battlefield is no place for a woman.
- Criteria of Development: After documenting the financial and social pitfalls of women in combat, I will analyze the military

implications of a co-ed battlefield.

These three (or four, or five) criteria of development (financial, social, and military) preview the essay's arrangement, providing the reader with a rhetorical road map for negotiating the complex terrain of the argument. They further assure that the thesis will not only be concretely developed, but that it will gather strength as it unfolds. The gain in clarity, concreteness, and comprehension more than compensates for the loss of suspense. The result will be an introduction that is a model of effective brevity--one that fulfills the promise of all three moments of an essay's beginning: that gets the reader's attention, emphatically announces an opinion, and unveils the criteria by which that opinion will be developed.

Student Example
> "In this essay, I will analyze the pragmatic elements of Isocrates' teaching philosophy, before comparing them to Dewey's pragmatic educational philosophy. Before I go further, however, it is useful to have a common understanding of pragmatism."

Analysis: By announcing not only the criteria for developing a thesis, but the order of that development (in short, by revealing the argument's arrangement), the writer heightens the reader's comprehension—one of the primary goals of an argumentative essay.

Rhetorical Strategies: The Criteria of Development

As with the attention-getter and thesis statement, there are several simple, yet practical strategies to use when previewing your criteria of development:

- You can simply mention them in the order in which you will write about them: weakest-to-strongest.
- If using this rhetorical structure, you can use a simple series of transitional words to introduce each criteria: first, second, third.
- Another series of useful transitional phrases with which to intro-

duce your criteria of development is the following: "After examining A, I will analyze B, before developing the relevance of C."
- You can also group your criteria with single transitions for each group, as follows: After analyzing the significance of A & B, I will develop the relevance of C & D.

Example: **Women in Combat**

"Before analyzing the importance of economic factors, I will assess the significance of constitutional and military arguments."

Example: Shakespeare's *Titus Andronicus*

"First, I will analyze Shakespeare's use of imagery; second, I will develop the significance of his subversive view of monarchy; and finally I will assess the extent to which the plot is informed by the conventions of the Elizabethan Revenge Tragedy."

Writing-to-Learn: The Criteria of Development
- In your journal, make an entry in which you list several criteria for developing your thesis;
- Limit these to the three or four most useful;
- Rank in reverse order, from weakest to strongest;
- Craft a sentence or two, previewing these criteria, using the rheotorical strategies modeled in this section;
- Share in group;
- Group provides feedback, noting strengths and weaknesses, offering suggestions for revision;
- "Recorder" compile a master list;
- "Reporter" share with class;
- At home, revise this "preview of criteria," incorporating any useful feedback from the group.

Writing to Learn: The Introductory Paragraph
- In journal, combine the attention-getter, thesis statement,

and criteria of development into an effective introductory paragraph.
- Share in group.
- Group provides feedback, noting strengths and weaknesses, offering suggestions for improvement.
- At home, in journal, type a final draft, incorporating any useful feedback from the group.
- Turn in for grade.
- Add to writing portfolio.

Introduction: (student sample)

Women At War

As enemy helicopters advance over the top of a mountain peak, your squad hunkers down for protection. You know you are on the verge of being fired upon. So you press your face deeper into the Iraqi desert. You dart nervous glances at your squad members, preparing for the fight of your life. You find yourself staring at the only female in your squad, wondering if you're hit, will she be able to carry you to safety. Your fears intensify. Instead of concentrating on the enemy, you're worrying about an even closer danger: the combat readiness of a squad member. While certain arenas of combat are suitable for women, a battlefield requiring close physical combat is not one of them. In the first half of this paper I will discuss training methods and minimum physical requirements. In the second half, I will rebut the argument that equal rights is more important than our soldiers' safety, before concluding with a search for common ground on this controversial issue.

Assessment/Conclusion

This introduction effectively captures all three "moments" of an essay's beginning: the opening garners the reader's attention and announces the focus; the middle concisely and emphatically states an opinion; and the end states how that opinion will be developed, while serving as a transition into that development. By practicing the rhetorical strategies modeled in this chapter, you too can learn how to craft effective introductory paragraphs to your academic papers, which fulfill several objectives at once, as follows:

- To arouse the reader's interest with an effective combination of attention-getters:
    1. the central research question(s)
    2. a quote
    3. a key definition
    4. a graphic fact
    5. a scene-setter
- To succinctly, yet emphatically state a thesis (opinion).
- To preview the criteria by which that thesis will be developed, and the order in which they will be developed.

Having aroused the reader's interest, stated what you will argue, and how you will argue it, it now only remains to prove or develop your argument.

CHAPTER FOUR

Depth Analysis and the Second Moment of Persuasion

Preview

This chapter models strategies for developing a thesis with the following:
- Personal experience
- Refutation of counter arguments
- Logic (depth analysis)
- Quotes
- Facts and stats
- Figurative language (metaphor, alliteration, sensory detail)
- Stylistic devices (transitions, dramatic verbs, heightened diction, parallel constructions, repeated phrases, lists, bullets, hyphens, colons, dashes, parenthetical phrases, etc.)

This chapter also models strategies of arrangement that heighten the persuasive impact of your argument:
- Weakest-to-strongest
- Shortest-to-longest
- Personal-empirical-analytical

The Purpose

An effective paper develops a given thesis (focus) from angles as diverse as they are substantive. Through the invention and discovery strategies already modeled, the writer has by now discovered the most productive means of developing a thesis. As with the introduction, in order to write effective body paragraphs for an academic essay it is imperative to first understand the purpose of the body—and then *write to that purpose* always and forever. If the purpose of an introduction is to get the reader's attention, state its thesis (emphatically and succinctly) and preview the criteria for developing that thesis (subheads), then the purpose of the body is to *concretely develop* that thesis. As noted above, there are several effective (and essential) means of developing a thesis.

Depth Analysis I

The first of these is the most important—and should always be the first (and last) line of development—the other strategies of development operating in support of it. Why? For the simple reason that it is "play of mind" that the reader most wants to see and is most effectively persuaded by. An essay is much more than just a collection of quotes strung together like items on a laundry line. While the voices of others (especially if they are authoritative voices on the subject at hand) are no doubt effective in supporting your view (opinion), it is YOUR view, your voice that the reader most wants to encounter. Your logic, your reasoning, your analyses, and your counter arguments will bring that intellectual voice into play, assuring its prominence in an essay where quotes, facts, and stats operate in support of that rational voice. Therefore, a good place to begin the development of a thesis is with a simple "laundry list" of the reasons you hold the opinion you do. Try and think of as many as you can, then rank them from weakest-to-strongest, and develop them in the same order.

This phase of the process is where "depth analysis" of a text comes into play, further highlighting the "play of mind." *Analysis* is simply the *process of breaking something down into its component parts:* if it is a literary text, those parts might consist of the theme, plot, characters, figurative language, generic integrity, narrative point of view, use of contrast, irony, myths, satire, etc. If the text under analysis is a print or television ad, those component parts are comprised of the hook, selling points, tag-line, color scheme, logo, and a host of selling strategies (bandwagon appeals, sensory appeal, sexual appeal, celebrity testimony, metaphorical associations with nature, healthy, beauty, and/or babies, etc.). If the text is an op-ed piece, its component parts might consist of a host of rhetorical strategies: logic, quotes, rhetorical questions or hyperbole, facts, figurative language, emotional appeals, repeated phrases, etc. If writing about a film, you might analyze its directing, acting, cinematography, editing, musical score, etc. If writing about a restaurant, you might analyze its food, atmosphere, service, etc.

Whatever the particular subject of the academic inquiry, analysis of that subject requires breaking it down into its component parts. By breaking a given subject (or text) into its component parts and then assessing the relative significance of each, the writer infuses a paper with the requisite "play of mind." Thus, at this stage of the writing process it is useful to borrow a page from Aristotle's play-book: *division and classification* of a particular subject into its component parts can help access the "deeper grammar" of a topic. This strategy naturally privileges (and develops) the ability to *think associatively*, to discover the relationship between widely scattered words, and herd them together, into their respective groupings (criteria/subheads).

Divide (or subdivide) and Conquer.

Writing to Learn: The Criteria of Development

(This sequence reinforces activities modeled in Chapter One).

Group-work: Criteria Development

- In your group, devise a list of writing topics (serious and/or playful).
- "Recorder" compiles master list of topics.
- Group selects a topic for collaborative practice.
- Individuals make a laundry list of *criteria* for developing this topic.

- This list is shared with the group.
- "Reporter" compiles a master list of criteria.
- Group radically limits the list to the 3 or 4 most important criteria.
- Group ranks these criteria from weakest-to-strongest.
- "Recorder" provides the "reporter" with this list.
- "Reporter" shares with class.

Group Work: Criteria of Development and Columnar Organization

A second means that affords collaborative practice in criteria of development is as follows:

- As a group, select a topic.
- In his or her journal, each member makes three columns, headed "Criteria," "Evidence #1," and "Evidence #2," as follows:

| **Criteria** | **Evidence #1** | **Evidence #2** |

- Under the column for "Criteria," list the categories that will be used to analyze the topic.
- Under the column for "Evidence #1," list evidence based on personal experience or direct observation for each criterion of development.
- Under the column for "Evidence #2," list the quotes, facts, or stats that pertain to each criterion of development.
- Share in group, filling in columns with overlooked evidence provided by peers.
- Volunteers share with class.
- Rank the criteria in column #1, weakest to strongest, with a numbering system.
- Rank the evidence in columns #2 and #3, in the same manner.
- Radically limit the criteria and evidence you would use, eliminating the weakest from each column.

- Share with group.
- Volunteers share with class.

Sample Topic: Analysis/Evaluation of Restaurant

Criteria	Evidence # 1 (pers. exp/obs)	Evidence #2 (sources)
atmosphere	noise level, lighting, privacy	review, field interviews
food	sensory details (taste, smell), presentation, pricing, portion	review quotes, field int.
service	timely, intrusive, personable	review, field int.

Climactic Arrangement of Criteria: 3-2-1 Organization

Having developed a rich body of "relevant intelligence" through the processes of free-writing and rewriting, of research and development, the moment inevitably arrives where it is necessary to begin exerting control over this mass of information—at which point the focus shifts from discovery and development to arrangement. At this stage of the process, cutting and pasting begins in earnest, guided by a system of division and classification that privileges associative thinking and climactic arrangement. The various fragments of "relevant intelligence" are grouped associatively under their respective criteria, which are then given a climactic arrangement, from weakest to strongest. Criteria of development (sub-heads) are numbered from 1 to 3 (or 4 or 5, as the case may be): 1 being assigned to the strongest, and 3 (or 4) to the weakest. These sub-divisions of development are then simply *cut and pasted* to reflect this linear progression in argumentative strength.

The criteria by which you develop a thesis emerge in two ways. Some become readily apparent *before* your start writing/researching. Others emerge during the writing/researching process. At some point, however, it becomes necessary to radically limit the scope of your inquiry to the most important criteria of development, and then decide on a tentative climactic arrangement of them (weakest to strongest). This done, you can then begin cutting and pasting the research quotes, free-writes, reader-responses, and marginal graftings, to their respective criteria of development, commencing with the first (or weakest).

Example

Pretend, for the moment, you are writing a paper on whether women should be allowed in combat. Let's assume, for the sake of argument, that your thesis is that women should NOT be allowed in combat. Let's assume you've settled on three primary criteria for developing this thesis: military reasons, economic factors, and constitutional rights. Let's further assume that, while compelling, the constitutional rights category is the weakest of your three. Let's also assume that your military reasons comprise the strongest category of the three. A simple 3-2-1 arrangement then would involve a sequence of criteria that commenced with the constitutional arguments, proceeded to the economic arguments, and (leaving the strongest for last) concluded with the military arguments. Such a flow of persuasion should build in strength as it proceeds, setting up the conclusion, in which the argument reaches its climax through a host of rhetorical strategies, including elevated diction, figurative language, climactic assessment, and an apt "clincher" sentence.

The Ladder of Persuasion

To achieve its goal (persuasion), an argument needs to climb a ladder of persuasion. It is useful to think of an argument not as a reductive "five paragraph essay," but as a continuum of persuasion, consisting of several distinct and definitive "moments." In writing such an argument, it may help to envision it as follows:

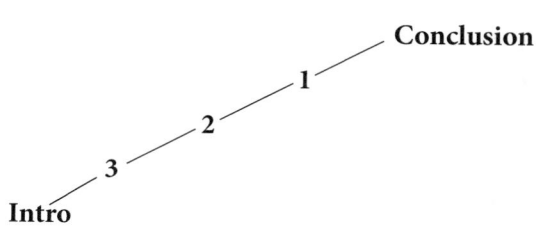

Now, this structure may prevail in a 5-7 page paper as well as in a 15-20 page paper. We are not referring to individual paragraphs here, but collections of paragraphs within a particular sub-category of thesis development—in which each criteria of development may be several pages long.

Writing-to-Learn: The First Pass

Sequencing (Harvesting) Marginal Graftings and Reader-Response Entries

At this point, it is necessary to roll up your sleeves and begin doing something about all the words scribbled in the margins of photocopied articles and course texts, or in your reader-response journal entries. Not to despair, for the other hard work of discovering useable content has already been done. Now you just have to retrieve, categorize, and transcribe it. This can seem like a Sisyphean labor in itself—but the work is as rewarding as it is unavoidable, as the body of your essay begins to take shape, to emerge from the mass of unorganized data. These are your first efforts in organizing this mass of supporting material into linear form, beginning with those graftings, quotes, and reader-responses that relate to your first criteria of development (sub-head).

- At home, in your journal, make an entry in which you use the first criterion of development from your introduction as the "heading" (write it at the top of the page).
- Begin retrieving/extracting the labeled marginalia (as well as the quotes to which they refer) from photocopied research sources and course-texts, *with page references.*

This final point is crucial, as it will save you frantic moments at deadline-time trying to track down the page reference for a quote you cannot afford to delete (which you must do, if the page reference cannot be found).

- Under the criteria-of-development heading in your journal, transcribe these marginal notes and source quotes.

- Work your way through the source, chronologically, extracting these marginal graftings and source quotes, transferring them to your journal, under the criteria-of-development heading.
- Under each "heading" you will soon have several pages of related "graftings" and quotes.
- If the process becomes too cumbersome for the length of your paper, then just extract and transfer what you deem to be the most significant graftings and quotes for your thesis.
- Do the same with the most relevant entries from your reader-response journal, which includes entries on those sources checked-out from the library.
- By the time you are finished, you will have your first draft of the material related to your first criteria-of-development, consisting of your marginal graftings, the quotes to which they refer, and your reader response entries.
- Photocopy a page from your journal.
- Share in group, narrating your process, identifying your thesis and first criterion-of-development, reading one of your transposed graftings or reader-responses.
- Volunteers share with class.
- Repeat this retrieval and transcription process for all criteria-of-development, until you have retrieved enough material to prove your thesis, including the most relevant or significant graftings and reader-responses.
- As the deadline approaches and as your paper approaches its desired length, it is sometimes necessary to do what is done in hospital emergency rooms: implement a "triage" system, in which you objectively assess the worth of any given grafting, quote, or reader response, "admitting" only those which must be saved, and omitting the rest.

This is where the time you invested writing in the margins, labeling marginal graftings, and responding to quotes in your journal pays dividends. With respect to the academic paper-writing process, it puts you ahead of the game: of peers who may be just starting to respond to source material, to discover what they think—whereas you have already developed pages of substantive content in the margins of your sources and the entries of your journal.

Writing-to-Learn: The Second Pass

Cutting and Pasting (Writing-to-Associations)

Having transcribed the material for a particular category of development, it is now necessary to start organizing it into some effective sequence of persuasion. Cut and paste skills, at this point, become very useful—and are greatly facilitated when working in an electronic (computer) medium. An effective labeling system in tandem with cut and paste skills is an effective combination.

- Make a pass through your criteria "column," identifying related graftings, quotes, and reader responses with a system of symbols.

- Then cut and paste, grouping like with like. You might, for example, group together all the material related to your personal experience, or to refuting the counter arguments. You might number the entries in the "column" weakest to strongest, and organize them accordingly, either saving the strongest for last, or eliminating the weakest altogether.

- Always be vigilant for the serendipitous association, which may until now have gone unnoticed, or that entry (or group of entries) that might make for an effective climax to this criterion of development; or that entry (or series of entries) which seems like a logical place to commence developing this criteria (subhead). You will develop a *felt sense* for arranging things in sequence (beginning-middle-end) both within a particular criteria and between respective criterion, both on a micro-rhetorical and macro-rhetorical levels.

- Repeat this cut and paste process of arrangement with the material in each criterion "column."

Writing-to-Learn: The Third Pass

From Arrangement to Writing

- Having grouped your column entries from weakest-to-strongest or beginning-middle-end, put the entries of each group into paragraph form.
- This affords further opportunity for rearrangement of the entries within a particular paragraph. Thus, be vigilant for these opportunities. Again, a well-honed, *felt sense* of arrangement is a very useful ally at this stage.
- In writing an academic paper, the arrangement process begins on the macro level and proceeds to the micro level. Thus, not only are the categories of development organized-to-climax, but the paragraphs within each category and the sentences within each paragraph are similarly sequenced for climactic effect. Consequently, the climactic arrangement on the micro level is replicated on the macro level, though the actual process of this arrangement occurs in reverse order: macro to micro. With respect to climactic arrangement, you begin with the big picture (the criteria of development) and gradually work your way to smaller and smaller units of arrangement (paragraphs, sentences within paragraphs, and finally words within a sentence).
- Transitional sentences, transitional words, and emphatic word order assist in this process of climactic arrangement.
- Also, be vigilant at this stage for opportunities to further rearrange the order of these paragraphs, for effect—the desired effect being a heightened persuasive impact. Organize to climax within a "column" of development, and between them.
- To modulate your argument from sentence-to-sentence and paragraph-to-paragraph, start working transitions into your writing. These add clarity and emphasis—in the process further heightening the impact of your argument. A simple transition, such as "most significantly . . . ." can add emphasis and clarity to your main point: the one that clinches an entire sequence of evi-

dence with climactic immediacy. Master the use of transitional sequences, as follows.

Example For example . . . further . . . and finally. . . .

Example First . . . additionally . . . most importantly . . . .

- This process of heightening the emphasis and clarity of your argument with transitions will, of course, continue in subsequent drafts. It is useful, however, to begin writing for emphasis and clarity now, which are a function of your arrangement and diction (including transitions).
- Adding a transitional sentence at the end of paragraphs, and at the end of this whole sequence, as a bridge into your second criterion of development, is an effective strategy insofar as it lends clarity, fluency, and emphasis to your writing (and the argument building within it).
- Complete this "arrangement-into-writing" draft for each criterion of development, writing a paragraph from each sub-group of related graftings, quotes, and reader responses, further reorganizing the sentences within a paragraph and the sequence of paragraphs as opportunity and insight allow, selectively adding transitions to reinforce the rhetorical coherency of your writing.
- Photocopy 2 pages.
- Share with group, narrating your process, identifying the criteria of development, the organizational changes you made to the order of sentences and paragraphs, the transitions you used.
- Group responds, noting strengths and weakness, providing suggestions for further reorganization, additional transitions, deletions, etc.
- Note: the focus of feedback at this stage is on the "deeper grammar" of the paper, not its surface level correctness (spelling, run-ons, fragments, etc.

Conclusion

By the end of this process, you will have "harvested" the most relevant material from your research, organized it into an effective sequence, and written it up in paragraph form. You now have a complete draft of a fully-developed, thesis-driven paper, sans the conclusion and works cited page. The writing, however, is still only in "rough" form. It is now time to take it to the next level.

Writing to Learn: The Fourth Pass

Writing for Scholarly Impact

In this pass though the body of your paper, you are writing for upgrades everywhere. You are cutting the weakest or excessive portions, amplifying the best (adding strength to strength), deepening the analysis as insight allows, looking for missed associations (and, therefore, still cutting and pasting for effect), bolstering weak paragraphs with further development, even adding a touch of color with an apt analogy, or an alliteration that springs to mind. In short, you are looking to improve your writing, word-to-word, sentence-to-sentence, paragraph-to-paragraph.

In places, your paper will shrink, thanks to a well-honed editing eye that is quick to detect mediocrity and excess. In other places, it will grow, as new avenues for developing your thesis or explicating a quote become suddenly apparent. The writing becomes smoother and more elevated at the same time, marrying clarity and content, adding style to substance, while everywhere you are looking to say 20 words in 10. By contracting in some places and expanding in others, your paper begins to acquire a uniform level of density, a substantive consistency, heightened here and there by flashes of your best analysis and most inspired writing.

It is in this critical pass that you must transform yourself from a mere arguer into a writer. All of these strategies will enable you to make this transition:

- Arrange material for climactic emphasis, at the paragraph,

sentence, and word level: that is, paragraph-to-paragraph, sentence-to-sentence, and word-to-word.
- Cut and amplify.
- Cut n' paste, grouping like-to-like.
- Say 20 words in 10.
- Selectively add transitions for fluency, clarity, and emphasis.
- Bolster under-developed paragraphs with more examples or more explication of given examples.
- Deepen the analysis where necessary or as additional insights allow.
- Search for gaps in your logic, avenues of developing your thesis you have missed.
- Bolster your refutation of the counter-arguments.
- Add a concise and compelling paragraph tying your personal experience into your argument (if relevant), and search for the right place to include it (usually the beginning of your body).
- Infuse some color into your analysis, with an analogy or an alliteration.
- And, lest I failed to give it its proper emphasis, say 20 words in 10: first, always, and forever.
- Of all the virtues of academic writing, clarity of meaning is the foremost. This form of writing privileges prose that is lean, clean, and mean. Lucid, attitudinal, and substantive. Analysis demands clarity of language, which in turn favors a "less-is-more" style. So strive for 10 words that say as much as 20. Always. Always. Always.

Evidence-based inquiry that is heavy on analysis and interpretation of the evidence will assure that your writing, instead of skimming along the surface of a topic, engages it in a substantive manner. Consequently, *depth of analysis* is the objective in this middle phase of the journey. Though quotes are an effective means of persuasion, insofar as they support your own claims and interpretations with expert (or otherwise compelling) opinions and hard evidence, what the reader most wants to see is not the play of another's mind, but the play of your own intellect: analyzing, interpreting, or responding in a substantive manner to other texts or opinions; logically developing a particular focus. Your marginal graftings and reader response free-writes will insure that your writing has this requisite *play of mind*—which is strengthened when you further develop these graftings and free-writes, and the significance of a particular quote, during the "writing moments" of this fourth draft. While essential to your development of a thesis, these quotes, facts, stats, figurative language, and relevant personal experience should be used in support of your own analyses—never as a substitute for it: They not only lend credence to your argument, but diversify the development of your thesis. It is the *play of your own intellect*, however, while reasoning, refuting counter-arguments, explicating a quote, developing its significance, or assessing the significance of a particular argument (including your own), that the reader most desires (and needs) to see.

Writing-to-Learn: The Pre-Final Pass

Writing-to-the-Finished-Product

Another way to heighten the effect of your writing is to selectively upgrade the diction (word choice) for emphasis and scholarly tone, by making a "diction pass" through your pre-final draft. A pocket thesaurus is a very useful, if not essential, writing supplement at this point. Simply select a key word or two in each paragraph, and upgrade it for a more scholarly or emphatic word. This will not only elevate the scholarly tone of your argument, but add emphasis at key points. Selectively adding a well-chosen, multi-syllabic word here and there will heighten the impact of your argument on the reader, insuring that your writing will achieve that "climactic" effect. Caution: do not overdo it. The goal is to heighten the effect, not brow-beat the reader to death with a Funk and Wagnalls. Pomposity undermines persuasion. A tone that is accessible, but scholarly and emphatic, is the ideal to shoot for.

This one-two combination of a climactic arrangement and emphatic diction is often sufficient to insure that an argument is written-to-climax. When capped by a conclusion that elevates the writing style and adds a touch of climactic assessment, the writing is more apt to reach its desired destination. The climactic arrangement of an argument throughout its body culminates in the elevated diction and climactic assessment of the conclusion, assuring that the paper is written-to-climax not just in its parts, but as a whole. What Marge Piercy observes of any "thing worth doing well," applies with equal veracity to the persuasive essay, which similarly

> has a shape that satisfies, clean and evident.
>
> Greek amphoras for wine or oil,
>
> Hopi vases that held corn . . .
>
> were made to be used.
>
> The pitcher cries for water to carry
>
> And a person for work that is real.

Like the amphora, the vase, or the pitcher, a well-crafted, persuasive essay "has a shape that satisfies, clean and evident." Further, what work could be more "real" than words that persuade an audience: whether that audience is a jury, a patient, a voter, a consumer, or your local congressman.

Development with Facts/Stats

In addition to logic, analysis, and quotes, facts and stats can be another effective means of developing your thesis. These can be integrated into your development throughout the body, as necessary, to support or clinch a claim you have made. Another effective means of developing your thesis in this manner is to include a short paragraph in which the facts and stats are concentrated: a *"just-the-facts"* paragraph, as follows:

Example: Student Paper on Manatees (Species Extinction)

West Indian Manatees are large aquatic mammals with grey bodies and a flat tail. They have two flippers. Their face is wrinkled and they have whiskers on their snouts. It is believed Manatees evolved from plant-eating, swimming animals. They are related to the Stellar's sea-cow—hunted until its extinction in 1768. An average adult is about ten feet long and weighs from 800-1500 pounds. Statistics released by Save the Manatee Club show that "there have been 4,672 manatee mortalities documented in Florida from 1974-2002":

> Of those, 1164 were attributed to water-craft collisions, 174 were attributed to flood gates or canal locks, 125 were other-related, 967 were prenatal (dependent calf), 191 were natural cold stress, and 625 were other natural causes. For the remaining 1426 carcasses no cause of death was identified: in the majority of cases, the carcass was too decomposed to determine cause of death. (19)

If presented in a concise manner, such a fact-based passage can be an effective means of persuasion: it not only lends substance to your case, while giving the reader some much-needed background information, but establishes your credibility as an arguer who has done his or her research. Such a compact paragraph adds weight and impact to your argument.

Writing-to-Learn: Development with Facts

- In your journal, make an entry in which you write a draft of a "just the facts" paragraph, extracted from your research.
- Photocopy and share in group.
- Group provides feedback, noting strengths and weakensses.
- Volunteers share with class.

Follow-up

- At home, in journal, write a separate, free-standing sentence for each fact of your *"just the facts"* paragraph, for practice integrat-

ing quoted material into your own text. Use the four strategies modeled in Chapter 2 for integrating quotes: author: quote/ quote: author/ quote-author-quote/ and "key word" quote.
- Share in group.
- In your journal, type a final version of a "just the facts" paragraph.
- Turn in for grade.
- Place in your writing portfolio.

Development with Personal Experience

Another effective means of developing your thesis is with personal experience—where relevant, and if handled concisely. It not only gives a strong *subjective voice* to the paper, which complements the objective analysis and presentation of quotes and facts, but heightens the reader's interest as well. How much more interesting it is to read a compelling and concise account of a personal experience related to the topic than a collection of facts, statistics and quotes. This of course violates one of the most outmoded, yet damaging rules of composition that teachers have historically foisted on students: never use "I" in a critical essay. In my view, it seems hypocritical of teachers to demand writing that "has a strong critical voice" while at the same time forbidding students to use "I." This is a rule which, like any, can (and should) be broken selectively, for effect. The best essays in my opinion have always featured a compelling and effective blend of subjective and objective writing. Infusing an *anecdotal account* of your personal experience, where relevant to your thesis, can be a very effective means of developing that thesis by adding concreteness to it and by heightening the effect on the reader, as evidenced by the following student sample, culled from an argumentative paper on the recreational use of wilderness areas:

> Growing up in the Northwest, skiing and sledding trips into the Cascades were a favorite winter pastime. In spring and summer, we'd go hiking. On both occasions we had to share

> the outdoors with snowmobiles and four-wheelers. The incessant whine from the engines and the plumes of exhaust were simply a fact of life, a necessary irritation. Usually I tried to ignore it—unless I was cut off in mid-path, showered with tire mud or had the tops of my skis run-over. For many years I had a "live and let live" attitude. The outdoors was big enough for everyone, right? Then I had a series of conversations with my roommate, an environmental studies major who has been looking at desert eco-systems for the past four years, that changed my thinking. True, plans are in place to improve emission standards and encourage more responsible usage, but these plans will do nothing to alleviate the real problem caused by off-road vehicles, especially in the desert: surface soil erosion and the air pollution that results from it. As an asthmatic with an extreme sensitivity to dust, I do not feel my health should be jeopardized to protect another's recreational hobby.

Be vigilant in developing any given thesis for points of intersection with your own experience—as long as this experience truly informs the topic and is *integrated succinctly* into it. A brief development of a thesis with a facts-only paragraph, with personal experience, or with the most cogent counter-arguments can be an effective means of beginning the developmental phase of your argument (the body), while sustaining the interest aroused by the attention-getter in the introduction. All too often in arguing a position we adopt a "just the facts, ma'am" approach based on the assumption that our own experience has no place in the debate. This prejudice is, I believe, a hangover from our love affair with the scientific mode of inquiry (objectivism) which privileges the assumption that subjectivity clouds objectivity (pathetic fallacy). Consequently, we favor the objective to the exclusion of the subjective—as if there was any such thing as a non-subjective objectivity. We have been taught to put our own subjects (and our subjective experience) under "erasure," as it were. By so doing we deny ourselves an effective, compelling, potentially interesting means of developing a thesis. Granted, the preponderance of development will rely on quotes, facts, statistics, logic and depth analysis. Nevertheless, there is room in such an argument for personal experience as well. Indeed, a sense of balance between objective-subjective writing would seem to demand it. Therefore, be vigilant in developing any given thesis for points of intersection with your own experience—as long as that experience truly informs the topic and is woven concisely into it.

Refuting the Counter Arguments

- At home, in journal, make an entry in which you list the counter arguments to your thesis (culled form your reader-response journal or your marginal graftings, where you have identified these con-arguments in your sources).
- Share list with group.
- Group adds to list with overlooked con-arguments.
- "Recorder" compiles a master list for each member.
- "Reporter" selects one and shares with class.

Follow-up

- At home, in your journal, make an entry in which you write a brief refutation to each con argument on your list.
- Combine your refutations of these con arguments into a paragraph (or two).
- Photocopy and share in group.
- Group provides feedback, noting strengths and weaknesses, offering suggestions for improving.
- At home, type a final draft of your con-arguments paragraph and your refutation paragraphs.
- Hand in for grade.
- Place in writing portfolio.

Conclusion: The Refutation of Counter Arguments, the Just-the-Facts, and the Personal Experience Paragraph(s).

Whether as points of departure (first criteria of development) or as shorter categories of development inserted between longer criteria of development to diversify your argument and to heighten the effect on the reader, these three, brief modes of development are very useful, if not essential to a well-argued thesis. A succinct recapitulation of the counter-arguments serves as an effective launching pad into your own argument, infusing a strong argumentative voice into the paper at the outset. A compact, just-the-facts paragraph can not only add substance and impact to your argument, but serve to break up the lengthy development of a major criteria of analysis, heightening the interest of the reader. Finally, developing your thesis with personal experience can be another effective means of beginning the body of your argument—if done concisely. It will give your writing a strong, subjective voice to complement the analytical and objective voice that builds your argument in the ensuing criteria of development. Informing your thesis with relevant personal experience also heightens the interest-level of the reader. If aptly handled, it will effectively set-up the rest of your argument.

These then are four effective means of **concretely** developing any thesis (quotes, facts, personal experience, the counter arguments)—as long as you remember that logic and depth analysis, because they foreground "play of mind," should always and forever be your first line of development. Because it is the most important and essential means of developing a thesis, I would like to further develop the strategies of writing-for-depth-analysis.

Depths Analysis II: Explicating Quotes

The purpose of explicating (or developing the significance) of any primary or secondary source quote is to further develop your thesis, to add depth of analysis to your argument, and to instill a little "play of mind" into your writing. Though the most significant part of the quoting process, this is (alas) the most often neglected. Whether from ignorance or sheer laziness of mind, some arguers write as if all they have to do to prove their thesis is quote from a text and then move on to the next quote. In so doing, they miss the *richest, most original, and therefore most convincing* means of developing their thesis: the one that really brings into play not someone else's intellect (as quoted), but their own, in the act of *interpreting a quote's significance* or relevance to their thesis. In the three-step process of introducing a quote, then rendering it exactly as written, and then developing its significance to your thesis (the "so what?"), the novice writer all-too-often stops after the second step—thereby omitting the most important phase of the process, and the deepest means of developing a thesis. On the other hand, by explicating the hidden meanings of a given quote, your writing will acquire that depth of analysis which is the foremost virtue (if not the *raison d' etre*) of any academic paper, and without which it has no compelling justification for being written at all. This error of omission critically flaws an argument by confining it to the surface of the source text, by assuring that it never gets beyond the common shallows of a text into its deeper *grammar*—where unexcavated meanings reside, waiting to be discovered.

Depth Analysis: Explicating Quotes

Interpretation is the essence of academic writing. Through interpretation, an essay grows beyond concrete development (through quotes, facts, stats, or personal experience) into depth of analysis. This is where an argument acquires and reveals its intellectual depth. Absent substantive interpretation of texts, an essay devolves into a mere collection of quotes, which for all their concrete engagement of a text, never penetrate its deeper grammar, plumb its unwritten depths.

To reach the deeper level of a text's meaning it is not enough to read its lines, but to read between them as well, to note the significance not just of what has been said, but of what has been left unsaid: to explicate its additional meanings, contradictions, limitations, rhetorical patterns, figurative language etc. The gaps in another's words invite our own. These spaces between the words invite us to partake of their hidden meaning, to participate in the meaning-making process, to co-author (if you will) the meaning of a given text, by continuing, if not completing, the process of its decoding. Additionally, well-written texts do not surrender their meanings easily (that is, at a glance), nor in their entirety. Such texts invite and reward scrutiny—if we know how to interrogate them and are vigilant for the associative wisdom they contain. An inquisitive mind, a vigilant eye, and a faith that additional meanings inhere in the words are all useful allies in this crucial "moment" of the writing process. Once found, recovered, and presented in ink, these interpretations of meaning are wholly your own—and add a signature quality to your writing.

Writing-to-Learn: Explicating Quotes

To break the habit of superficial engagement with a quote, of merely integrating it into your text and then moving on to the next quote, begin the sentence immediately following the quote with the following phrase: *"This quote is significant because. . . ."* This is particularly useful, if not essential, after a block quote, which if important enough to be quoted at length in the first place, usually contains meanings that invite, if not insist upon, further comment. To leave these hidden meanings lying on the table, as it were, is an egregious error of omission, insofar as it subverts the primary goal of your paper: to *demonstrate play-of-mind through depth analysis in support of a thesis.*

- In your journal, make an entry in which you integrate a quote into your own words, with proper attribution. Begin the next sentence with, "This quote is significant because . . . ," and complete the sentence: looking for ways to tie the quote to your thesis, to assess what it adds to an argument, what it reveals about a character, how it develops a central theme, or relates to previous passages or anticipates others. Note: not every quote will lend itself to this additional explication of its significance, so be vigilant for those quotes that invite further commentary, qualifica-

tion, clarification, or explication of their meanings: that possess a density or complexity of meaning that necessitates some reading-between-the-lines, as it were.
- Follow the same procedure with a block quote, beginning the first sentence after you have integrated it into your own text with the words, "This is significant because...."
- If you strike it rich, you may find yourself writing more than one sentence, perhaps even more than a paragraph of *explication*. By all means, let your pen write until it exhausts itself because this "moment" of writing is the essence of effective academic writing, in which the reader sees you responding critically and analytically to another's words, in which he or she sees the *play of your own mind* in response to another's.
- Photocopy and share in group.
- Group provides feedback, noting strengths and weaknesses, adding suggestions for improving the explication, providing responses that may have been overlooked, etc. Again, the focus of this feedback is on the deeper grammar of the writing, not its surface level correctness.

Follow-Up

- At home, in journal, rewrite your explication of this quote, incorporating any useful suggestions from the group.
- In your journal, make an entry in which you first identify five quotes from your research, using either your marginal graftings or reader-response entries, worthy of further explication. Record each at the top of a page, and explicate its significance or relevance to your thesis.
- A final word: a paper with quotes that haven't been explicated for their significance is somewhat akin to a photo album whose negatives haven't been developed. This want of *concrete development*, this absence of *depth analysis* can be fatal to an argumentative paper. An argumentative paper is not the place to be "dallying in the shallows" of a topic or another's words (Piercy, "To Be of Use").

What might this explication-of-quote-process look like in action, on the page of a paper?

Allow me to use an example from my own academic writing to illustrate the process.

Example (From *Words in the Wilderness*, 72):

> Freire's analysis of the effects of colonization . . . also attests to the dual, conflicted world the oppressed inherits:
>
>> There is also an unnatural living death: life which is denied its fullness. Oppression dualizes the 'I' of the oppressed. Thereby making him ambiguous, emotionally unstable, and fearful of freedom. Part of the oppressed 'I' is located in the reality to which he adheres; part is located outside himself, in the mysterious forces which he regards as responsible for a reality about which he can do nothing. He is divided between an identical past and present, and a future without hope. (173)
>
> *Freire's observations here are significant* inasmuch as they "unveil," if only partially, the underlying causes of apathy manifested in borderland learners. His observations echo as well the findings of Adams and Hogan with respect to the "cultural disorganization" or "disintegration" experienced in this extremity of bicultural alienation. The extent to which the psychic and emotional world of the Other is destabilized by the experience of marginalization depends on the degree to which identity remains rooted in one culture or the other; its most debilitating effects, however, are evidenced in those students for whom identity is rooted in neither culture.

By pausing to reflect or comment on a quote's significance, the effective arguer avoids the pitfall to which many novice academic writers succumb: superficial engagement with another's text or words. These responses to another's text add depth of analysis to the writing, taking the paper where it consistently needs to go during the development of a thesis. By practicing this simple, yet effective rhetorical strategy, you too can give your academic writing that depth analysis which alone does justice to the genre, which alone justifies the investment of time and the expenditure of ink. Such analysis justifies the existence of an argumentative essay, which without it, devolves into a mere academic exercise.

Writing-to-Learn: The Reader Response Journal

- Return to an entry in your reader response journal, to a quote that invites further commentary. Pick up where you left off, beginning your response with the words "This quote is significant because . . . ."
- Photocopy and share in group.
- Volunteers share with class.

Explication by Interrogation

Another useful strategy is to begin your explication of a quote's significance by asking a question (or series of questions). If they are the right questions, they will lead you to the "deeper grammar" of a quote's meaning. What might this process look like in action? The following explication of a passage from Shakespeare's *Romeo and Juliet* (a common first-year reading) is illustrative of the process.

Juliet's ACT III address to the night in Shakespeare's *Romeo and Juliet* is a useful passage to model development-through-depth-analysis (or play-of-mind through explication of a quote). This passage so deeply informs her character and the drama's central themes that it invites and rewards a closer reading:

> Gallop apace you fiery-footed steeds/toward Phoebus' lodging: such a wagoner as Phaeton would whip you to the west /and bring in cloudy night immediately . . . . /that runaway eyes may wink, and Romeo/leap to these arms. . . . Come civil night/ thou sober-suited matron all in black. . . . Hood my unmanned blood beating in my cheeks/ with thy black mantle, till strange love grows bold. . . /Come, gentle night; come loving black-browed night/ Give me my Romeo, and

when I shall die/ take him and cut him out in little stars/ and he will make the face of heaven so fine/ that all the world would be in love with night. (III. 2. 1-27)

A passage like this is so rife with significance an entire paper could be written on it alone—which is why you needn't analyze (or even comprehend) a text in its entirety. You merely need to zero-in on those passages dense with possibilities of diverse meanings or those otherwise relevant to your thesis. An academic paper, at most, offers a *selective* (as opposed to a comprehensive) analysis of a text. A series of rhetorical questions prompt and guide the writer's response to the text. Begin, by asking yourself the following:

- What does this passage reveal about Juliet's character?
- How does it reinforce the play's major themes or develop its central conflicts?
- How does the imagery inform the meaning of the passage and the drama in general?

Let's begin with the middle question first. A brief analysis of Juliet's words reveals how Shakespeare reinforces the plot's central theme through speech: "gallop apace," "whip you," "immediately," and "leap to these arms" all develop the theme that "haste makes waste." Critics have correctly cited the lovers' amorous hastiness as their tragic flaw. Here, Juliet's words give voice to that heedless and headlong pursuit of passion, come what may. Shakespeare's imagery similarly reinforces the primacy of passion's speed. For example, he compares Juliet's desire to "fiery-footed steeds" and to Phaeton, the "wagoner [who] would whip you to the West." The hot immediacy of a desire that will brook no delay is similarly suggested by the "blood beating in my cheek."

What then is the significance of Juliet's words and Shakespeare's imagery? They reveal that in the brief, but violent struggle between Juliet's virtue and her passion, between her loyalty to the Capulets and her love for a Monatgue, that the tide has turned decisively in favor of her passion—all the more fitting as this speech occurs in Act III, traditionally the turning point in a Shakespearean tragedy:

the point at which the protagonist ceases to be the master of his (or her) own fate, and becomes a plaything of a destiny preordained by his or her own tragic flaw. In the case of the youthful lovers, that flaw is a passionate impetuosity that consigns them to a premature grave. Their end is truly tragic insofar as it arouses a sense of unmitigated and unnecessary waste, as do the deaths of Hamlet and Othello, driving home to the reader (or the audience) the sad lesson that amorous haste does indeed make waste.

Not enough depth of analysis? Let's proceed even deeper into the text's meaning, see if we can "plumb one yard below" Shakespeare's words. Again, let's begin with a question: how does Shakespeare's imagery reinforce this theme that romantic haste makes waste?

Shakespeare's dark and deterministic imagery not only unifies this passage, but also deeply informs the play's central theme that romantic haste makes waste. The images of "night" serve a dual dramatic function: they allude not only to a night that will provide a cover for the lover's intimacies, but foreshadow their tragic end by previewing that "night" into which their love will blindly lead them. The image of the "West" is steeped in this duality, not only as a herald of the night that will unite them in love, but as a harbinger of the "night" that will unite them eternally in death. "Curtain" similarly gestures toward an immanent intimacy as well as toward the "final curtain" of life. Even the image of Romeo's lover's "leap" into Juliet's arms is invested with suicidal connotations, heralding his passionate leap into the embrace of death. The image of "amorous rites," likewise is invested with a subliminal fatality, conjuring images of pagan virgin sacrifices on a sacred altar, opening negotiations with the beyond, and suggesting that Romeo and Juliet, like sacrificial scapegoats of ancient Greece, were offered on the altar of love to purge the community of its violent crimes, to appease the gods, and to restore peace. Recall, that the Greek word for tragedy is "goat song": a reference to the cleansing sacrifice of a goat.

Conclusion/Assessment

Again, this is a mode of development that can be honed with practice, by free-writing in response to quotes in a reader-response journal. By keeping such a journal, the academic writer can get a jump on the writing process, excavating texts for their "deeper grammar," taking these "practice swings" at explication. Often, the gems of an original interpretation that form the centerpiece of an academic essay are found in these exploratory textual excavations. It doesn't hurt to come to the academic writing process with the diligent curiosity of a rock-hound, or an archeologist of meaning-making. And like those diggers after knowledge, you too must play the "believing game." Peter Elbow advises hidden meanings have less chance of remaining hidden when confronted by inquisitiveness, hard work, and faith in their discovery. Under the allied pressure of these things, a text is more likely to surrender some, if not many, of its meanings.

That said, it is just as true that no interpretation can ever "lay out" a text's meaning in its entirety. The interpretative act is, by definition, selective and partial. The goal is not to "lay out" a text's meaning once and for all, but simply to add to the possibilities of its meanings.

This technique of analysis can apply to any text, upon whose latent and multiple meanings rhetorical questions are brought to bear, as a springboard into a deeper analytical engagement with it:

- What is it leaving out?
- What are the limitations to the argument it is making?
- What are its contradictions?
- How does its figurative language reinforce its claims?
- On what underlying assumptions is it based?
- How does it resonate with other passages, other texts?
- What interpretations or arguments has it overlooked?
- What does it contribute to the on-going debate?

The number of questions a writer can pose to a quoted passage are limited only by the richness of his or her imagination. In time, you will develop a "felt sense" for knowing which questions to pose to any given passage, to access its deeper grammar. All it takes is two or three of these explicated passages to produce a paper rich in depth analysis. How much easier it then becomes to write a paper that deeply analyzes several block quotes, than one that must find one- or two-dozen quotes that it briefly explicates, if at all. Depth analysis rewards the writer in more ways than one: it not only significantly heightens the effect on the reader, but actually makes your job of writing easier insofar as it privileges quality over quantity: quality of analysis over quantity of quotes. In this sense, too, less is more. The trick in reaching your end is not to write to the end, but to write to the depths. For by writing to the depths you will achieve your end: and you will achieve it long before you reach the end.

Explication: Writing-in-the-Margins

Let's look at a second example to illustrate the process, explicating a blocked quote, in this instance the same passage from Plato's *Phaedrus* that I used to model the invention strategy of "grafting" in the margins of a text (see next page). The passage is an interesting commentary on the psychological dynamics of the master-pupil relationship in ancient Greece: a relationship on which our contemporary education model is largely based. As is often the case, the "deeper grammar" of a text can be accessed by posing a question or two to yourself to focus the analysis, as follows:

- What is the meaning of Plato's text (Socrates' speech)?
- Is Socrates speaking literally or ironically?
- Using this speech as an example, what are we to conclude is the purpose of rhetoric: seduction, persuasion, or performance?
- And what, as our question asks in the right margin, is the relationship between love and rhetoric?

An initial reading of Socrates' speech could well contend that he is here laying out a definition of good writing: division and classification, definition and summary. Covino (whose interpretation follows this passage) challenges this literal interpretation, offering a more provocative reading: the meaning of the passage is not to be understood literally, but ironically. Far from saying what he means, Socrates is "performing" Phaedrus' rote summary of Lysias' speech about love (as my "grafting" in the l. margin observes). He is modeling Phaedrus' own uncritical mimicry of Lysias' text, by speaking like Phaedrus, as a pretext for exposing Phaedrus' own "critical blindness to ambiguity" (Covino 140).

Before Socrates can model his own critical reading of Lysias' text, he models Pheadrus' uncritical summary of the text, which he will then dismantle—as part of a two-fold process intended to raise Phaedrus' critical consciousness regarding Lysias' text: in order to elevate Phaedrus' pseudo-knowledge to knowledge (see bottom margin). Socrates, among other things, is modeling a teaching methodology, as well as a mode of critical inquiry.

This level of interpretive response is not achieved in the original marginal grafting. There isn't room or time: it is, rather, achieved afterward, when these graftings are gathered and transferred to the empty page of your reader-response journal. I simply begin with the one in the left margin (L1), transferring it to an empty page, whose heading it becomes:

Ex/ L1: "Soc. mouthing Phaedrus' orality, a vehicle for consuming Ph. Satiric pastiche."

Free-write: Then I simply free-write in response to this grafting, elaborating and further developing its meaning, its relevance to the quote.

Then I move to the next grafting, repeating the process. In this fashion, I free-write on each of these marginal graftings, to amplify my analysis of the passage. Questions posed to myself drive the analysis:

Questions

- Might there be more to Socrates' words than this—other possible meanings?
- What, for example, might be the deeper psychological implications to Socrates' "performance" of Phaedrus?

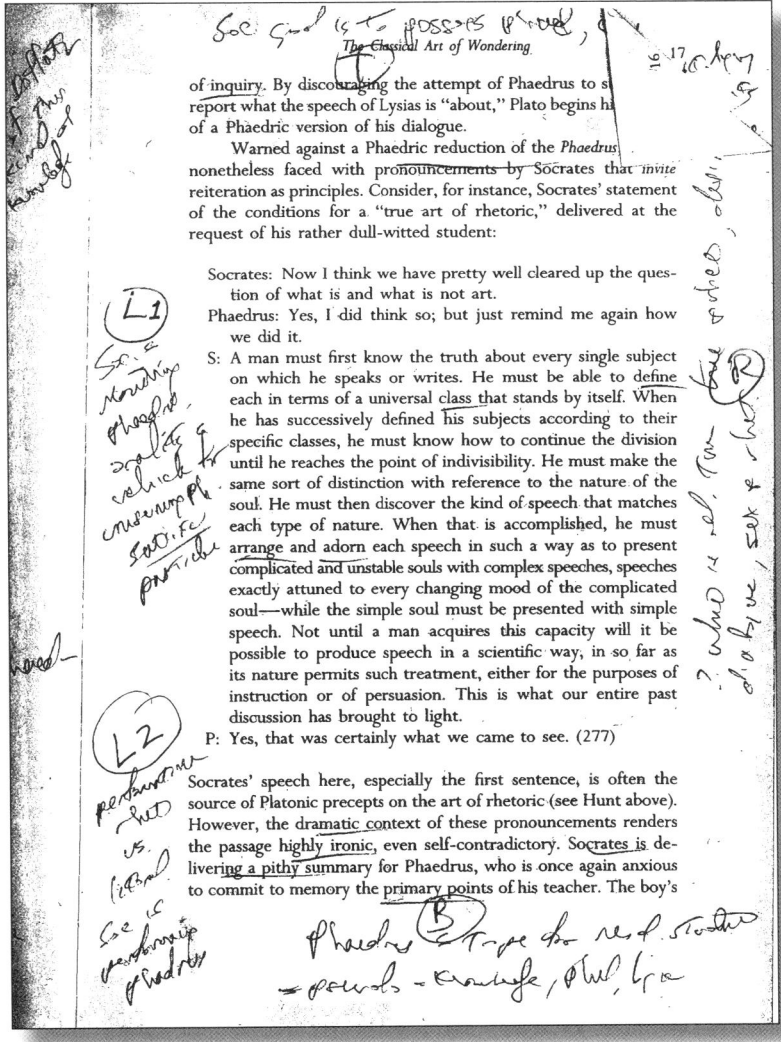

Explication

We might assert, for instance, that Socrates' "performance" of Phaedrus evidences a predatory desire of the Self to assimilate the Other, by mastering its thought and speech patterns. We might further assert that Socrates' desire to possess Phaedrus' mind arises from a desire to possess him physically—or the opposite: that the seduction of Phaedrus' mind is intended as a form of foreplay, whose ultimate goal is the seduction of his body (top margin grafting). Recall, that the subject of Lysias' speech is love, and that to the Ancient Greeks the origins of Logos (or discourse) were deeply rooted in Eros: the desire for physical beauty leading to a desire for beautiful ideas. In other words, Logos and Eros are inseparably yoked in the rhetoric of the ancient Greeks. In order to assimilate Phaedrus, Socrates must first convert himself into a facsimile of Phaedrus, by thinking and speaking like him—so he can then perform the even greater task (and his true objective) of converting Phaedrus into a facsimile of himself-as-critical-thinker-philosopher (left margin grafting).

An inquiring mind might discover even further psychological implications of this rhetorical take-over/make-over, having to do with the soul's quest for immortality. Socrates, in converting Phaedrus into a facsimile of himself, is seeking to eternalize his own soul in that of his student. This desire to eternalize the self lies at the heart of the master-pupil relationship in Ancient Greece: dialectic rhetoric being conceived not only as a vehicle for discovering eternal truths, but for eternalizing the soul of the master in the pupil, as evidenced by the Socrates/Plato, Plato/Aristotle, and Aristotle/Alexander-the-Great relationships. Thus, as the passage suggests, the purpose of rhetoric is not merely seduction, persuasion, or performance, but a combination of all three.

The meanings of these marginal graftings are developed (or elaborated) once transposed to the empty page, further deepening the interpretive analysis of the text in question. Recognizing which passages relate to your thesis, identifying those that invite further commentary, and knowing which questions to pose to them all serve as springboards into a deeper analysis of those passages. Marginal graftings and rhetorical questions that prompt freewrites in response to a text comprise an effective strategy for accessing its hidden and multiple meanings. It is in these original explications that the writer truly signs his or her name to an essay: a process that commences when the writer starts *questioning* a text, interrogating its meanings, in a quest to uncover a new meaning, to enrich the possibilities of its meanings, or to lend a hand in the construction of its meaning.

Writing-to-Learn: Writing-in-the-Margins

- Select a page from your course readings or Photocopied sources in which you have filled the margins with commentary. Transfer one of these marginal graftings to an empty page in your journal, preceded by the quote to which it refers (with page reference).
- Free-write, adding on to the marginal grafting, developing its main point, and further explicating the significance or relevance of the quote with respect to your thesis.
- Photocopy the original page and share in group, along with your free-write, explaining your marginal short-hand.
- Group provides feedback, noting strengths and weaknesses of the explication, ways to improve it.
- Volunteers share with class.

Follow-Up

- At home, in journal make an entry in which you transpose and free-write on the most important graftings from your research.

Explication: SITA (The Search for Inter-Textual Associations)

Wisdom is associative. Meaning does not inhere solely in a given text (or passage), but in its associations with other texts, or passages within a given text. Though we might analyze it as if it was an autonomous, free-standing fragment within the text, in reality it was created as part of a meaning-continuum. This invites further analysis—indeed, insists upon it. Having led us into the deeper grammar of a given passage, that search now leads us forwards and backwards in the text, for other passages that resonate with it.

Write not only to depth but to breadth, explicating a given passage of a text not only for its autonomous, free-standing significance, but for its intra-textual associational meanings. For it is only by seeing it in relation to other passages that its full meaning will emerge. The academic writer not only excavates meaning vertically in any given passage, but laterally: exposing associations between passages in a text. This ability to think associatively is one of the hallmarks of critical thinking: to think outside-the-box (as well as within the box) of a given passage. It is a critical component of any rhetorical analysis: to apprehend a passage (no matter how small) in itself, as well as in relation to other passages.

The Ladder of Persuasion: Mobilizing the Evidence

The first moment of the essay's body can be usefully devoted to a counter-argument paragraph, a personal experience paragraph, or a "just the facts" paragraph. Similarly, the second moment of the body can be usefully devoted to *mobilizing the evidence*—in a rhetorical drumbeat that gathers momentum as it proceeds from the weakest to strongest *criteria of development*. In other words, if in the first moment of development the emphasis is on the personal, then in this second moment of persuasion, the emphasis shifts to the empirical evidence. This is the "moment" where an argument, interpretation, or analysis needs to make its case, concretely. If need be, style can be sacrificed for substance. What is essential at this point of the argument is that a compelling body of evidence be presented in a systematic arrangement. One way to achieve this is to reserve the most substantive portion of your argument for this middle phase. Though style will heighten the effect of your writing, substance will carry the day for your argument. In this middle phase, quantity of evidence takes primacy over quality of style— though ideally both should be operating in tandem. Nevertheless, evidence that is lined out coherently, effectively linked, arranged for emphasis, and augmented by depth analysis will carry the day even sans a brilliant writing style. Clarity and concreteness will prevail with or without a graceful style. Consequently, think "substance" through this middle passage.

The writer needs at any stage of the argumentative journey to be able to write in various modes: for invention, arrangement, and finish; for focus, development, and climactic assessment; for color, concreteness, and correctness; for logical, emotional, and ethical appeals—for both style and substance. If the initial moment of the body can be devoted to the less important criteria of development, then subsequent moments of development are devoted to increasingly important criteria, emphasizing the quantity and quality of evidence. The most significant, original or otherwise compelling criterion of development should be reserved for the final moment of the essay's development. The best depth analysis should be reserved for this portion of the argument. Body of evidence can at this stage give way to depth of analysis, as the compelling mass of the previous moment gives way to the depths and insights of the final moment of the body.

If arranged for climactic emphasis, the argument should gather momentum as it unfolds. This defers until the conclusion, however, the clinching transformation from arguer to writer: at which stage style takes precedence over substance, assessment over evidence, pathos over logos, and color over concreteness. For an essay to reach its proper destination, the writer must know what that destination is. Summary is not the destination of an essay; climactic assessment and heightened effect are its true destination. An essay that ends in summary ends with a rhetorical whimper. Instead of being written-to-climax, such an essay is written to anti-climax.

Thud.

Review/Assessment

This chapter modeled strategies for developing a thesis, as follows:

- Refuting the counter-arguments
- Personal experience
- Facts
- Logic
- Depths analysis/ explication

- Marginal grafting free-writes
- Reader-response free-writes
- Multiple draft/ rewrites

It also modeled strategies of climactic arrangement, as follows:

- 3-2-1 arrangement of criteria of development (weakest to strongest; personal-empirical-analytical)
- Interior arrangement of each criteria for climactic effect (columnar)
- Arrangement by paragraph, sentence, word for climactic effect

Familiarity with these rhetorical strategies of persuasion will enable the novice academic writer to give a thesis-driven argument the development and organization, the substance and clarity, the emphasis and depth it deserves, and indeed demands. If added to the writer's rhetorical tool-kit, these strategies enhance the likelihood of enjoying a high level of success, not only in the marketplace of ideas that is academia, but in the marketplace of professions beyond.

CHAPTER FIVE

Climactic Assessment and the Final Moment of Persuasion

Preview

This chapter models rhetorical strategies for writing an effective conclusion—for "arriving," not just as an arguer, but as a writer, as follows:

- Restate the central research question.
- Assess the significance of your argument.
- Assess the implications of the counter-arguments and of your own thesis.
- Make a strong personal statement.
- Heighten the diction.
- Heighten the effect with some color (metaphor, alliteration).
- Heighten the style (parallel construction).
- End with an effective "clincher" (quote, play on title, a look toward tomorrow).

The Purpose

Having wrestled this Frankenstein of logic, quotes, facts, statistics, personal experience and textual analysis into a satisfying, linear, and climactic arrangement, you are ready to proceed to the final "moment" of persuasion: climactic assessment. The purpose of an essay's conclusion is **not** to restate the thesis and sub-heads, nor is it to re-hash your main arguments. The purpose of a conclusion is twofold: first, to add some *climactic assessment* of your argument's significance and implications: to answer the "so what" and the "what if?" aspects of your argument. Its second purpose is to *heighten the effect* of your writing upon the reader. There are several simple, yet effective rhetorical strategies for achieving each of these objectives.

Generally speaking, a conclusion that is "short and sweet" is more desirable than one that is an exercise in reductive redundancy—that merely restates your thesis and sub-heads, reviews or summarizes the evidence, and in effect says "that's all folks." Such a reductive and dysfunctional ending to a paper is not climactic, but anticlimactic: assuring that it ends, not with a "bang," but a "whimper." If you listen closely to such essays, you can almost hear the hot air hissing from the rhetorical balloon. Reading these strangulated endings is akin to watching an essay in its death throes—that has had the life choked out of it. A garden hose with a doubled-up crimp in the line.

If this is the problem, what might be the solution?

If, until now, you have devoted your time and space to effectively introducing, stating, and concretely developing your thesis, at this stage of the intellectual journey you need to "arrive" not only as an effective arguer but as a writer. A little style (and a few rhetorical touches) will go a long way toward realizing this goal. If until now you have relied on logic, quotes, examples, stats, facts, and personal experience to concretely develop your thesis, at this point a little "climactic assessment" and "color" are in order. Blending these two virtues in a conclusion will accomplish the goal of heightening the effect on the reader, assuring that your essay "arrives," not just as an argument, but as an effective piece of writing.

But how to accomplish this dual effect in your writing? Having developed your various criteria for climactic effect, how do you take a paper to yet a higher level of writing? The answer is not as difficult as you might imagine. What is required at this moment is a *retrospective glance* over what has been argued thus far: assessing the worth, originality, or implications of the argument. At this point, the writer needs to answer a simple question: *So What?* In tandem with a *few stylistic touches, a figurative device or two, and an apt quote, this climactic assessment* will go a long way toward fulfilling an essay's initial promise—and primary goal: heightening the effect on the reader. Following are a few rhetorical strategies designed to achieve these goals:

1. Re-introduce the *central research question* with which you got your reader's attention in the very first sentence.

2. *Assess the significance* of your thesis and argument, answer the "so what?"

   - What is so important or original about it? *Self-reflexively* assess the worth of your argument, by pointing out what it contributes to the scholarly debate, what gaps in our knowledge it fills, what new directions it takes the critical conversation. What new perspectives does it bring to bear on the issue at hand? What is so important about it that you spent an entire paper arguing it? Having arrived at the end of your argument, you are now perfectly situated to cast a retrospective glance of assessment back over it. So begin the ending by looking back.

   Writing-to-Learn: Assessing the Significance

   - In your journal, make an entry in which you cast a retrospective glance over your thesis, answering the "so what?" What is so significant about your argument? At this moment of your conclusion, you can also make a strong personal statement, writing passionately about your opinion (thesis).
   - Photocopy and share in group.
   - Group members note strengths and weaknesses, offering suggestions for improvement.
   - Volunteers share with class.

3. *Assess the implications* of your thesis for the future.

   - Having answered the "so what," answer the "what if." Having cast a retrospective glance of assessment over your argument, direct your gaze (and the reader's) to the future, assessing the problematic, if not dire, implications of the counter-arguments, as well as the positive implications of your own argument, by asking yourself a simple question: what might the world look like tomorrow if the con-arguments came true? Or conversely, what problems might be resolved if the opinion you are advancing became reality? Not every thesis-driven argument breaks new ground. However, every argument has value: therefore, the conclusion is the place to tout the importance and implications of your perspective. One way to do this, is to imagine "what if?" What if the contrary views were enacted into law? What might be the consequences?

Example: Censorship of Gangsta' Rap lyrics

Suppose you have argued against censorship of Gangsta' rap lyrics for their glamorization of violence. You might conclude by speculating on the dangerous and discriminatory precedent of censoring one form of artistic expression for other forms of artistic expression. If we censor Gangsta' rap lyrics today for their violent content, what might be censored tomorrow for a similar reason: John Wayne war movies? Saturday morning cartoons? Books? Films? Television? Indeed, what sort of America might we awaken to tomorrow if we start down the slippery slope of censorship today? In other words, if you begin your ending by looking back over your paper, end it by looking forward.

Example: The Global Warming Crisis

If we do nothing about the global warming crisis today, what sort of world might we inhabit tomorrow? A world with 30% fewer species? A world without polar bears? A Florida coastline that begins at Orlando, whose greatest attraction is no longer its mile-long beaches, but its two-dozen Atlantis'?

Writing-to-Learn: Assessing the Implications

- In your journal, make an entry in which you develop the problematic implications of the counter-arguments to your opinion, as well as the positive implications of your own view. Begin by asking yourself, "what might tomorrow be like if counter-argument A became reality?"
- Share with group;
- Group notes strengths and weaknesses, offering suggestions for improving, implications that may have been overlooked.
- Volunteers share with class.

4. Peroration (making a strong personal statement).
   - If, while assessing the significance and/or the implications of your thesis, you can do so in the context of a strong personal statement, waxing passionate or eloquent in your views, your writing will also take on a climactic tone, heightening the effect on the reader.

Writing-to-Learn: A Strong Personal Statement

- In your journal, make an entry in which you develop your opinion with a strong personal statement.
- Share in group.
- Group provides feedback on strengths and weaknesses.
- Volunteers share with class.

5. Upgrade the diction.
   - Heighten the effect on the reader by heightening the diction. Highlight a few words in your conclusion, click on thesaurus, and go shopping. Select a more intelligent-sounding word from the menu. At this final stage of the journey an apt, multi-syllabic word or two can heighten the scholarly tone of your writing, thereby heightening the effect on the reader. Caution: don't overdo it. A few key word upgrades will do (uh, make that "suffice").

- A scholarly tone is of course a desirable virtue to seek throughout your paper. However, if you upgrade your diction nowhere else, do it in your conclusion. This "spike" from middle-to high English will further heighten the effect on the reader, reinforcing the climactic tone of the writing. So, instead of writing "he *likes* her," you might write "he *venerates* her," or "he *reveres* her."
- To achieve this climactic effect, all that is necessary is to *selectively upgrade the diction*. This can be done with the essay as a whole during a *pre-final editing pass*, in which the writer selectively highlights key-words to upgrade. Instead of shambling along in middle English from beginning to end, the essay comes alive with these *scholarly spikes* in the diction, which similarly help it fulfill its scholarly promise.

Writing-to-Learn: Upgrading the Diction
- In your journal, selectively highlight a few key words in your conclusion, from your previous entries, and upgrade them for scholarly tone.
- Share in group.
- Volunteers share with class.

6. Add a little color.
- Another way to heighten the effect on the reader is to add (make that, "infuse,") a little color into your conclusion with a figurative device or two: with an apt metaphor (or analogy) or an effective alliteration. At this final stage, a touch of poetry can be a very effective means of persuasion, reinforcing the emotional appeal of your strong personal statement (peroration). *If the body of your paper relies primarily on an appeal to logos (logic) to persuade, then the conclusion relies heavily on an appeal to pathos (emotion) to persuade.* A little color in the form of a metaphor or alliteration can add a touch of style to your argument, thereby heightening the effect on the reader.

Writing-to-Learn: Writing for Color
- Find a place in your previous journal entries pertaining to

your conclusion and make an apt analogy (metaphor).
- Find a place where you can make an alliteration.
- Share in group.
- Volunteers share aloud.

7. Heighten the style.
   - Figurative devices are not the only means of heightening the style of your writing (and therefore heightening the impact on the reader). Another means is to craft a parallel construction or two.

8. Add a quotation.
   - An apt *quote* will also reinforce the scholarly tone and heighten the effect on the reader, the more so if it is also the final sentence of your paper, or the *clincher sentence.*

9. The clincher sentence.
   - The last sentence of your paper is every bit as important as the first, the last impression as significant as the first. It is absolutely imperative if you are to realize the goals of a conclusion that you have an effective clincher sentence—or effective exit line. These can assume several forms:

     1. The aforementioned *quote.*

     2. *A play on your title* (which underscores the importance of having an effective title). In this way, the final words the reader sees will return them to the first words they saw, completing "the loop" of your argument, as it were, reminding them subliminally of the ground you (and they) have covered since they first glimpsed these words in the title.

     3. A thought that leaves the reader *looking toward the future.*

Putting the Pieces Together

What might the results of this process look like? Following is a student sample of a problematic concluding paragraph, followed by a version that has been revised for climactic assessment/impact by my mentor, Prof. John Clark, of the University of South Florida.

Student Example

> "Each year, at each job, I became more outgoing and assertive. I feel these jobs have made me a better person. I was surprised at the results I saw in myself. I still find myself tongue-tied on occasions, but I am making progress every day and feel better about my personality."

Assessment/Analysis

Instead of ending the paper on a climactic note, this conclusion ends, not with a bang, but with a rhetorical whimper. Consequently, the effect produced on the reader is the precise opposite of that which is desired. Further, whatever persuasive effect has been gained by the introduction and body is lost by the anti-climactic effect of such a strangulated conclusion. Like those papers that end with a rote recapitulation of the thesis and sub-heads, and nothing more, the ending to this paper falls flat—and far short of the desired effect upon the reader. No matter how compelling an argument might be during its introduction and body, if it "flat-lines" at the end, much of its positive effect will be lost.

Perhaps the ubiquity of this problem is due to the fact that crafting effective conclusions to argumentative essays is an under-taught aspect of the process. The irony is, that with a few simple rhetorical strategies, this "flat-lined" conclusion can be turned into an ending whose last impression is as strong and engaging as the essay's first, as the following revision by Professor Clark evidences.

Revised Version

> "At that point, I suddenly discovered that *over the past few years I had come a long way:* I had escaped the *confining closet* of myself, but I had also begun, as any useful member of society must, to help others *emerge* from their solitude, privacy, and insecurity. *Emerson's* ideal of Self Reliance *com-*

menced paradoxically to work for me as well—only when the Self could rely upon others, was that Self strong enough to induce others to rely upon me."

This simple revision achieves all the goals, possesses all the virtues of an effective conclusion:

- Color (alliteration and metaphor): "*confining closet.*"
- Upgraded diction: "*commenced paradoxically.*
- Quote: *Emerson* on "Self Reliance."
- Style/Parallel constructions: "*I had escaped . . . helped others emerge. . . ;*" "*the Self rely upon others . . . others rely upon me.*"
- Climactic assessment: the conclusion effectively, and succinctly, articulates a retrospective judgment on what has gone before: *Over the past few years, I had come a long way.*

As Professor Clark's revision evidences, a combination of these rhetorical strategies will go a long way toward insuring that your paper is written-to-climax, that at the end of the journey you *"arrive" as a writer* in a manner that *heightens the effect* on the reader—adding the final persuasive nuances to your argument. The final word, I reserve for Professor Clark:

> Only by *continual evaluation, play of mind, and assessment* can a writer *coerce* an essay to *build inductively* toward a *poignant climax*. And only at the close can the student *truly assess* what has gone before. The last stage of the *journey* is the natural place for *peroration*, and therefore, at the finale, the student must learn to be more apt as a writer to *"arrive."* (my emphasis)

Writing-to-Learn: The Conclusion

In your journal, make an entry in which you combine the previous entries, selecting what is best, strongest, or most effective from each:

- Start by restating the *central research question.*

- Assess the significance, or "so what," of your thesis.
- Assess the implications of the counter-arguments and your own opinion.
- Selectively upgrade the diction.
- Add some figurative language (a metaphor or alliteration).
- Heighten the style with a parallel construction.
- Add an effective clincher (quote, play on title, look to tomorrow, etc.).

Follow Up

- Photocopy and share in group.
- Group provides feedback, noting strengths, weaknesses, and ways to improve.
- Type a final draft of your conclusion.
- Hand in for a grade.
- Add to portfolio.

CHAPTER SIX

Get it Write: Editing in the Writing Workshop

"Decades of research have shown that isolated grammar drills do little to improve student writing and are a poor use of instructional time."

—NCTE Press Release (Oct 24, 2006)

Preview: The Five Egregious Sins

In three decades of teaching composition at the high school, community college and university level, if there is one thing I have observed, it is this: novice academic writers tend to make the same five types of "errors." This hasn't changed much with time or geographic location, with grade level or academic setting. By eliminating these five problems from a paper, you can eliminate 80-90% of all editing mistakes. Further, improving the surface-level of your writing in five ways is *learnable* in a fourteen-week course. All it takes is the will and a little "hands on" practice. These editing errors are so common to novice academic writing that I call them the *five egregious sins,* as follows:

- Wordiness or awkward/unclear wording.
- Run-ons and fragments.
- Spelling.
- Punctuation.
- Subject/verb agreement.

This chapter provides hands-on practice in eliminating these editing errors from your final draft. Of the five editing "sins," by far the most problematic is the first: wordiness or awkward/unclear wording. How to reduce, if not eliminate, this problematic aspect from your academic writing? The solution is simple: learn to write 20 words in 10.

Less-is-More: Writing Twenty Words in Ten

Academic writing favors prose that is "lean and clean," in which clarity of meaning is the objective and economical use of language the means to achieve it. All too often, however, the meaning in a piece of novice academic writing gets lost amidst the wording, in the translation from thought to language. In this chapter, hands-on practice in these problematic aspects of academic writing is situated in the context of your writing, or in the context of everyday writing, as it actually is used in real-world settings—as opposed to situating this instruction in the abstract, de-contextualized setting of a grammar handbook. In this context, practice in editing takes on an immediacy, relevance, and interest that it lacks when confined to a grammar handbook.

The Editing Workshop: Writing-to-Learn

Foreign Signs/Rewrites

Listed below are some signs and notices written in English that were discovered throughout the world, which call attention to the problem of awkward, unclear, or wordy syntax.

In your journal, make an entry in which you revise each for clarity of meaning.

Example 1: In a Belgrade hotel elevator:

> To move the cabin, push button for wishing floor. If the cabin should enter more persons, each one should press a number of wishing floor. Driving is then going alphabetically by national order.

Example 2: In a Paris hotel elevator:

> Please leave your values at the front desk.

(The point to be made here is that spell-check won't catch this. Lesson for pre-final draft: spell-check, print, proof-read, correct, final print.)

Example 3: In a Yugoslavian hotel:

> The flattening of underwear with pleasure is the job of the chambermaid.

Example 4: In a Japanese hotel:

> You are invited to take advantage of the chambermaid.

Example 5: In an Austrian hotel catering to skiers:

> Not to perambulate the corridors during the hours of repose in the boots of ascension.

Example 6: In a Zurich hotel:

> Because of the impropriety of entertaining guests of the opposite sex in the bedroom, it is suggested that the lobby be used for this purpose.

Follow Up

- Share in group.
- Volunteers share aloud with class.

Letters to Welfare Department/Rewrites

The following sentences were culled from actual letters received by the Welfare Department. in application for support. In your journal, make an entry in which you *revise for clarity* as follows:

- Assume the role of the letter writer.
- Write a short letter (2-3 sentences) in which you clearly explain the circumstances and purpose of the letter.
- And in which you close with a tactful request for assistance.

Example 1: I am forwarding my marriage certificate and six children. I had seven but one died which was baptized on a half sheet of paper.

Example 2: I am writing the welfare dept to say that my baby was born two years old. When do I get my money?

Example 3: I am very much annoyed to find that you have branded my son illiterate. This is a dirty lie, as I was married a week before he was born.

Example 4: Unless I get my husband's money pretty soon I will be forced to lead an immortal life.

Example 5: In accordance with your instructions I have given birth to twins n the enclosed envelope.

Example 6: I want my money as quick as I can get it. I have been in bed with the doctor for two weeks and he doesn't do me any good. If things don't improve I will have to send for another doctor.

Follow Up
- Share in group.
- Volunteers share with class.

Student Samples/Rewrites (culled from papers):

Instructions: Line-out any unnecessary words, then rewrite for clarity. Work directly on the page.

Example 1: As far as getting ready for winter, I put anti-freeze in the car.

Revision: Every winter I put anti-freeze in the car (9 vs. 14 words, 33% reduction).

Example 2: The point should be made that American cannot afford to become an isolationist country.

Revision: America cannot afford to become an isolationist country (8 vs. 14 words).

Example 3: I might hasten to add that I don't agree with capitol punishment.

Example 4: Let me make it perfectly clear that in my opinion a person's right to privacy is not as important as the public's right to know.

Example 5: He is more or less a pretty outstanding person in regard to good looks.

Example 6: Fran said some insulting things, after which her friend became insulted.

Example 7: As a major in the field of economics I plan to concentrate in the area of international banking.

Example 8: Johnson's extremely significant research let to highly important major discoveries.

Example 9: Andy has a left fist that has a lot of power in it.

Example 10: The nature of her talent was very large.

Example 11: He really had more intellect than the others in his class at school.

Example 12: There are a number of items that might need to be considered at some length on the agenda.

Writing for Clarity/ The Paragraph
Instructions
- Working directly on the page, do a line-by-line edit of the sample paragraph below, lining-out words, substituting your own words, correcting misspellings, and re-punctuating as necessary.
- Type up your revised version.
- Photocopy and share in group.
- Group offers feedback on ways to strengthen each sentence.
- Volunteers share aloud with class.
- In journal, upgrade your revision, by selectively highlighting key words (verbs, for example) and using your thesaurus, replace with a more intelligent, if not multi-syllabic word.
- This enhances the scholarly tone of your final edit.

Sample Paragraph:
We all to some degree have both good and bad types of

characteristics and the bad ones usually stand out. The negative quality that stands out most in the person that I intend to describe in this essay is the one of her being too analytical. This individual is one who hesitates a lot and thinks things out too much to ever make some kind of decision. Of course, I may be wrong, but such a quality appears to be annoying. Her mind is not made up and some decision is never come to. There is however, a positive aspect of her analyzing everything and that is the fact that she avoids appearing haughty or overconfident. Still, she cannot make up her mind, get a point across, or come to some conclusion. She really irritates people that she comes in contact with, and most of her problems center around this possible fault.

Example 1 (lst Sentence.): "We all to some degree have both good and bad types of characteristics."

Revised version: We all have good and bad characteristics.

Upgraded revision: We all *possess* both good and bad *traits*.

Analysis: By reducing the excess verbiage (8 vs. 13 words), and by selectively upgrading the diction ("have" to "possess" and "types of characteristics" to "traits"), the meaning has not only become clearer, but more emphatic.

Example 2 (lines 1-2): "and the bad ones usually *stand out.*"

Revision: "but the bad ones are usually more *apparent.*"

Complete Revision: We all possess both bad and good traits, but the bad ones are usually more apparent.

Upgraded Revision: We all *harbor* good and bad traits; the bad, alas, usually *prevail.*

Analysis: "Possess" and "more apparent" have been selectively upgraded to "harbor" and "prevail," adding emphasis and further heightening the scholarly tone, without sounding pompous or pedantic. The diction has been further tightened from 16 to 12 words (25%) by a simple upgrade in punctuation from a comma to a semi-colon, further heightening the parallelism of the two sentences. Hence, the simple progression from "have" to "possess" to "harbor" heightens the effect and the scholarly tone of the writing, as does the progression from "characteristics" to "traits." By learning to write 20 words in 10, and by selectively upgrading key words in each sentence, you are adding two key virtues to your academic writing: clarity and scholarly emphasis. The goal is twofold: to selectively and sequentially tighten and upgrade the wording, to line-out unnecessary words and to climb a ladder of diction. The diction upgrade is made easier with the invention of the electronic thesaurus. All you have to do is highlight a key word (verbs are good places to begin), click on the thesaurus, and go shopping for a more scholarly sounding one.

Note: I owe a debt of gratitude to my mentor, Professor John Clark (University of South Florida) for modeling this form of writing-for-clarity and emphasis.

Revised Paragraph (Sentence by Sentence)

Sentence 2: *The negative quality* that stands out most in the person that I intend to describe in this essay *is the one of her being too analytical.*

Revision: *Maria's worst characteristic* is *her habit of excessive analysis.* (9 vs. 26 words)

Sentence 3: This individual is one who *hesitates* a lot and *thinks things out too much to ever make some kind of decision.*

Revision: She *regularly hesitates* and *scrutinizes too much* to ever make *a* decision. (12 vs. 21 words)

Sentence 4: Of course, I may be wrong, but such a *quality appears to be annoying.*

Revision: Of course, such a *flaw is annoying.*

Sentence 5: Her mind is not made up and *some decision is never come to.*

Revision: She cannot know her mind or *be decisive.* (8 vs. 13 words)

Sentence 8: She really *irritates* people that she comes in contact with and most of her problems *center around* this *possible* fault.

Revision 1: She *irritates* every acquaintance and most of her problems *derive* from this *crippling* fault.

Upgrade of Revision: In short, Maria *infuriates* her friends and *rattles* strangers, but that's entirely her own fault: the *sore spot* on her personality is a *self inflicted wound*.

Writing to Learn: Paragraph Revision

- Type up your final, upgraded revision.
- Share in group.
- Turn in for grade.
- Add to portfolio.

Writing for Clarity: Business Letter/"Downtown Real Estate Agency"

Instructions: Beginning with sentence 3 (first line of the letter below), line-out any unnecessary words. Be prepared to justify each deletion.

Example Sentence 1: "We here at the Downtown Real Estate Agency, located for your convenience in beautiful downtown Springfield, are at present time conducting a search for our first personnel computer, with which we will begin implementing the computerization of our operations.

Revision 1: "The Downtown Real Estate Agency is conducting a search for our first personal computer, in order to computerize our operations." **(20 vs. 40 words)**

Justification of Deletions

- "We here at the" (redundant);
- "located for your. . . . Springfield" (appropriate for a travel brochure, but irrelevant for a business letter);

TO: The Citrus Computer Corp.: 400 Pueblo Rd.: Scotts Valley, CA 96066

FROM: Downtown Real Estate Agency

We here at the Downtown Real Estate Agency, located for your convenience in beautiful downtown Springfield, are at the present time conducting a search for our first personnel computer, with which we will begin implementing the computerization of our operations. We need one that is above all else versatile, while still retaining it's features of economy. To maximize our technological ability to the fullest possible extent. While doing the search a new computer form your company was announced. Enclosed herewith please find a copy of an ad that you, the Citrus Computer Corporation, placed in the magazine entitled "Business computing." The ad says, to write to you for info. Before I go any further here, let me make perfectly clear that we will need software for word processing, graphics, do you also have what's called a spreadsheet package (for the financial stuff)? Could we get this computer fixed locally if something goes wrong with it? Do you give a warranty? We want to avoid getting a computer that is frequently inoperable. The point here is that it seemed to me that your computer would be just the thing for us, but calling around to all the stores, they said the Tangerine 2000 isn't out yet: that's the name of the computer I'm talking about. I'm really in a bind here, because we need a system that's sophisticated yet easy to learn for some of our people—especially our girl who does our typing, etc.—experiences feelings of intimidation when dealing with machines that are highly technological. Also, how much does all this cost, your ad doesn't even say. We had narrowed our choice down to two other personal computers but your looks like it might be better and we want to get the latest thing so we decided to check to make sure. Therefore I hereby request that your company, the Citrus Tangerine 2000, send us information. In case there's any confusion, I'm enclosing that ad to clear everything up. Please find it enclosed herewith. Also, how long would this computer last in the normal course of events? Please reply at an early date, and in addition let us know which stores in our area will have it when

> it does come out, because that's certainly important. The main thing we are wondering, is will someone come to our offices to set things up and train us?
>
> With warm personal greetings, I remain, Yours respectfully,
>
> E.T. Whizen, Office Manager, Downtown Real Estate Agency
>
> P.S.: What kind of printer can you get with this Tangerine 2000? I don't want to have to have to get one of those cheap deals that some guys use, the appearance of letters is extremely important if your in business. If you have any questions, please don't hesitate to call!

- "are at present time conducting" (wordy, redundant).
- "conducting" is in present tense.
- "personnel" (wrong word).
- "with which we will begin implementing the computerization of" (wordy).

Upgraded Revision 2: "The Downtown Real Estate Agency is searching for its first personal computer. **(12 vs. 40 words)**

Justification: "in order to computerize our operations" (redundant).

Analysis: This upgraded revision is a much clearer statement of the letter's purpose, succinctly set forth in the opening sentence.

Follow-up

- Revise lines 6-11 from "We need one. . ." to "'Business Computing,'" working directly on the page.
- Share revisions in group.
- At home, revise the rest of the document, working directly on the page.
- Type up a revised version, incorporating all your editing chang-

es. As part of your final revision, cut and paste, looking for opportunities to group similar sentences together, enhancing the clarity and organization of the letter.
- Turn in final edit for grade.

Example: Successful Revision

> The Downtown Real Estate Agency is in the market for a personal computer. We are seeking a PC that is versatile and economical. We have several *software needs*, as follows: word processing, graphics, and a financial spreadsheet package. Additionally, could you respond to the following *questions* regarding the Tangerine 2000 model:
>
> - when and where will it be available?
> - price?
> - warranty?
> - most compatible printer?
> - where serviced?
> - training of staff provided?
>
> Many thanks for your kind attention.
>
> Sincerely,

Conclusion/Assessment

Similar contextual practice in editing to eliminate the other egregious sins (run-ons/fragments, spelling, punctuation, and subject/verb agreement can also give your final draft the level of correctness it needs (and deserves).

By eliminating these five types of editing problems from your writing, you will eliminate the most problematic of its surface mistakes. Though your goal is always to produce a word perfect paper, perfection is something we rarely achieve—in writing, as in most any other endeavor. It is, nonetheless, a goal worthy of our aspiration; for in seeking perfection, what you often find is mere excellence—and the success or satisfaction that come with it.

Works Cited

American Library Association. "Information Literacy Competency Standards for Higher Education." *Presidential Committee on Information Literacy: Final Report*. Chicago: American Library Association, 1989.

Brown, Stephen Gilbert. *The Gardens of Desire: Marcel Proust and the Fugitive Sublime*. New York: SUNY P, 2004. ---. *Words in the Wilderness: Critical Literacy in the Borderlands*. New York: SUNY P, 2000.

Clark, Carol Lea. *Searchers: A Quick Guide to Researching, Evaluating, and Documenting Electronic Sources*. Southlake, TX: Fountainhead, 2005.

Covino, William A. *The Art of Wondering: A Revisionist Return to the History of Rhetoric*. Portsmouth, NH: Boynton/Cook, 1988.

Crowley, Sharon. "Teaching Invention" in *Strategies for Teaching First-Year Composition*. Ed. Duane Roen, et al. Urbana, IL: NCTE, 2002.

Derrida, Jacques. *Dissemination*. Trans. Barbara Johnson. Chicago: University of Chicago P, 1981.

Elbow, Peter. *Writing Without Teachers*. New York: Oxford UP, 1973.

Fulwiler, Toby. *The Working Writer*. 5th ed. New Jersey: Prentice Hall, 2006.

Greenblatt, Stephen. *Will in the World: How Shakespeare Became Shakespeare*. New York: W.W. Norton, 2004.

Kershner, R. Brandon. *James Joyce: A Portrait of the Artist as a Young Man*. Ed. Kershner. New York: Bedford, 2006.

Lefevre, Karen Burke. *Invention as a Social Act*. Carbondale, IL: Southern Illinois UP, 1987.

Neel, Jasper. *Plato, Derrida, and Writing*. Carbondale, IL: Southern Illinois UP, 1988.

Pizer, Donald. *American Expatriate Writing and the Paris Moment: Modernism and Place*. Baton Rouge: Louisiana State UP, 1996.

Plato. *Phaedrus*. Trans. H.N. Fowler. in *The Rhetorical Tradition: Readings From Classical Times to the Present*. 2nd ed. Eds. Patricia Bizzell and Bruce Herzberg. New York: Bedford/ St. Martins, 2001: 138-168.

Rank, Otto. *Beyond Psychology*. New Jersey: Hadden Craftsmen, 1958.

Shakespeare, William. *Romeo and Juliet* in *The Complete Works of William Shakespeare*. 5th ed. Eds. by David Bevington. New York: Pearson Longman, 2004.

Vygotsky, Lev. *Thought and Language*. Trans. Eugenia Hoffman and Gertrude Vakar. Cambridge, MA: MIT P, 1962.

Williams, Joseph. *Style: Ten Lessons in Clarity and Grace*. 7th ed. New York: Longman, 2003.